Electronic Portfolios:

A Guide to Professional Development and Assessment

Marilyn Heath, Ed.D., NBCT

**Your Trusted
Library-to-Classroom Connection.
Books, Magazines, and Online**

Library of Congress Cataloging-in-Publication Data

Heath, Marilyn.
    Electronic portfolios : a guide to professional development and assessment / Marilyn Heath.
        p. cm.
    Includes bibliographical references and index.
    ISBN 1-58683-099-6 (pbk.)
    1. Portfolios in education--Computer-aided design. I. Title.
LB1029.P67H42 2004
371.14 ' 4--dc22
                                            2004012666

Author: Marilyn Heath

Linworth Books:
Carol Simpson, Editorial Director
Judi Repman, Associate Editor

Published by Linworth Publishing, Inc.
480 East Wilson Bridge Road, Suite L
Worthington, Ohio 43085

ISBN: 1-58683-099-6

5 4 3 2 1

table of contents

figures

appendices

author biography

Marilyn Heath received her Bachelor of Science in Education and a Master of Arts in Geography from Bowling Green State University (Ohio). She received her MLIS and her Ed. D. from the University of South Carolina and has worked as a media specialist and educator for the past eighteen years. After receiving her doctorate in Curriculum and Instruction, she directed the Media Services program at East Tennessee State University. She returned to South Carolina to resume her work with high school students as a media specialist, and she became a National Board Certified Teacher in 2003.

Dr. Heath has written articles and presented at both state and national conferences on the topic of electronic portfolios; this is her first book. When she isn't working or writing, she reads and gardens. She has one adult son, Michael, and shares her home with her kitty, Gracie.

dedication

This book is dedicated to my parents, Paul and Laura Heath, who have given me a lifetime of support and encouragement.

acknowledgements

I would like to acknowledge the expertise and generous help of my son, Michael Whited, with the software descriptions in Chapter Seven. Michael, who works in technical support and Web page design, is the computer whiz in the family, and I owe much of my technology know-how to him.

I also thank Dr. Carol Simpson for her expert advice regarding the issues of copyright and trademark law.

Special thanks to Consulting Editor Sherry York and Editor Donna Miller for their assistance, support, and wise counsel.

I first became a media specialist in 1990, and at that time I knew very little about portfolios. However, it was not long before I realized that words on paper could not adequately describe the various aspects of the job I was doing. I began taking pictures—pictures of special displays, pictures of contest winners, pictures of visiting authors, pictures of conference activities, pictures of special events. In addition to my pictures, I had clippings of newspaper articles, letters of support and appreciation, certificates from training sessions, awards, and copies of publications. Eventually, I organized all of these artifacts into a binder, labeled them, and felt satisfied I had created an accurate and informative picture of my media center and my practice. Little did I know at the time I had made my first attempt at creating a professional portfolio.

At about the same time, the media specialists in my district were charged with the task of revamping our evaluation instrument. It had become clear the assessment used for teachers did not adequately measure the knowledge and skills necessary in the library. With much hard work, we developed a new assessment. It detailed pages of performances, arranged by standards, and was scored using a Likert-scale type of assessment. It did a better job than its predecessor, but it was still a generic, one-size-fits-all assessment that did not present a clear picture of what happened in the media center.

Although the new assessment instrument did a better job of reflecting knowledge and skills, I still felt it did not present a true picture of my professional self. I kept adding to my collection of pictures and other artifacts, and my binder got thicker and thicker. I even titled it Professional Portfolio of Marilyn Heath, but it would be several years before I realized that my first attempt at creating a professional portfolio fell short of the mark.

It was ten years later I first heard about electronic portfolios at a technology conference. After that, I made it my quest to find out all I could about professional portfolios, especially electronic ones. I researched, experimented with my own portfolios, wrote, and presented on the topic. The results of those endeavors come together in this book. It is not, however, a culminating experience. You will discover, as I have, that professional portfolios are never truly done—at least not until the end of our careers. Until then, we can keep learning, growing, and recording our progress in our electronic portfolios.

The book is intended to asist practicing educators, as well as pre-service teachers, administrators, and teacher educators, in their development of a professional portfolio, but the book concentrates specifically on reflection and how the reflection process in portfolio development contributes to professional development.

In addition to presenting the conceptual process of portfolio development, the book is meant to be a practical guide to portfolio development. Thus, the chapters are sequenced from the conceptual considerations before the portfolio is begun to the final polish of the completed portfolio. The book is a workbook in the sense that worksheets and step-by-step instructions are provided to help you through the process from start to finish. By the time you finish the book, you can have a completed portfolio. As you will learn early in the process, even a person with basic computer skills can create an outstanding professional electronic portfolio. Furthermore, you can do it all with software you probably have available to you right now.

However, this book is not intended to serve as a technical manual. Specific, how-to instructions for software programs or particular pieces of hardware are not included. It is expected that the user has or will achieve a functional level of expertise before attempting portfolio development. Discussions of software and hardware are meant to inform readers as to their appropriateness for portfolio development—nothing more.

With that said, a closer look at the book's contents is in order. The book identifies ten steps of portfolio development in five distinct sections. The first two chapters are included in Section One: Considering a Portfolio. This section of the book is conceptual, and the chapters examine what a portfolio is, why a professional portfolio is beneficial, and the advantages of choosing an electronic portfolio. With a firm conceptual grounding, the book moves on to explore various organizational considerations in the second section, Planning a Portfolio. This section looks at the importance of identifying the portfolio's purpose, identifying the prospective audience, and developing specific objectives.

Developing a Professional Portfolio is Section Three of the book, and each of the three chapters addresses a specific question that will help you develop your portfolio. This section helps to determine what your portfolio should include, your reflections on those artifacts, and plans for the future. Reflection is an integral part of an effective portfolio, and it is covered thoroughly here.

Section Four explores the issues to consider in Producing a Professional Portfolio. Hardware and software choices are explored, as well as the basics of good design. The final section of the book is Presenting a Professional Portfolio. This section suggests ways to present your portfolio to peers, students, administrators, and, of course, your portfolio's intended audience. It also reviews the portfolio process and provides a final check sheet and discussion of how to give your portfolio the final polish it needs to be flawless.

The book is organized to help you move through the portfolio development process step by step. Even if you are not fully convinced you need an electronic portfolio or are unsure you can develop one, the goal for this type of portfolio is professional growth; the process is every bit as important as the product if it is to help you achieve your professional goals. A good approach would be to read the first section to decide if an electronic portfolio fits your needs. If so, then continue with Section Two to consider organizational issues. If, at this point, you are convinced that you should develop a portfolio and feel confident that you can develop an electronic portfolio, then you are ready to begin.

You may copy and use the worksheets located in the appendices to help you through your own professional growth process, and don't forget the final, crucial step of checking your work to apply a professional polish.

Chapter One
What Is a Professional Portfolio and Why Do I Need One?

Portfolio development has been part of the educational scene for several years. Pre-service teachers often develop a portfolio as evidence that they have met professional standards and as a requirement for graduation. Later, a new graduate may use the same portfolio as a supplement to her résumé to land her first teaching position. Then, unless the educator is applying for National Board certification or some other achievement, that portfolio is put on the shelf and rarely, if ever, used again.

It is time to take a fresh look at portfolios. Portfolios have the versatility to offer a rich and authentic portrayal of our professional practice,and can be used in a variety of situations that require documentation of professional activities. Most importantly, no matter what their purpose, a portfolio provides the author with a unique opportunity for professional growth and development.

Defining a Professional Portfolio

Before considering an electronic portfolio, it is important to understand what a professional portfolio is and what it is not. We are familiar with the term in other contexts: Artists have portfolios, as do interior designers and architects. Investors have portfolios of stocks, bonds, and other assets. Very likely, we are also familiar with the term in the context of education: Our students develop portfolios over the course of the year or semester in order for us (and them) to assess the quality of their work and their growth over time. We might use their portfolios as a showcase of their best efforts or as a way to accurately convey their strengths and weaknesses to parents or other caregivers.

All of these types of portfolios have various elements in common. They are all collections of artifacts either created or owned by the portfolio author, all in a virtually constant state of flux as artists add new pieces, investors buy and sell, and students learn and grow, and all in a constant state of scrutiny, most importantly by the author, but by others as well. Interior designers display their portfolios to potential clients, investors sell high and buy low, and teachers grade and assess. Ultimately, all these portfolio authors want their portfolios to be truly representative of their best efforts.

The same can be said of a professional portfolio for educators. It, too, is a collection of artifacts that represents the author's best efforts. Over time, it will reflect the professional changes and growth of its author, and it will be examined, evaluated, and assessed by a varied audience.

What else should we know about a professional portfolio? Searching for a definitive description in literature leads to almost as many definitions as there are publications on the topic. However, most agree on the following characteristics:

- A professional portfolio is an *organized collection*. A professional portfolio must be organized so it displays the author's artifacts in the best possible light and in logical order so that the audience can make sense of the author's intentions.
- A professional portfolio contains *self-selected artifacts*. Self-selection is an important attribute because it allows the author to critically assess her own work and accomplishments and apply her professional judgment in selecting pieces to include in the portfolio. It allows the author to inject her own personality into the portfolio.
- A professional portfolio is structured around *goals and objectives or standards*. Goals and objectives or standards provide the organizational basis for the professional portfolio. Just as a carpenter would not build a house without a blueprint, an educator cannot construct an effective professional portfolio without a plan of how it will be developed.
- A professional portfolio documents a *variety of skills and knowledge*. Typically, a professional portfolio is developed to highlight knowledge and skills related to the goals and objectives or standards around which the portfolio is organized. In most situations, this requires a variety of artifacts.
- A professional portfolio is developed for a *specific purpose*. Purpose is one of the criteria by which artifacts are selected. Just as a focused piece of writing has a purpose, so does a focused professional portfolio.
- A professional portfolio is targeted at a *specific audience*. A focused professional portfolio is aimed at a specific audience, another criterion for selecting artifacts.
- A professional portfolio contains *reflections* on the artifacts collected. Reflections are the heart of a professional portfolio. More than any other element in the portfolio, reflections exhibit the author's ability to thoughtfully and critically examine her own work.
- A professional portfolio demonstrates *growth over time*. Growth over time should be the natural result of reflecting upon one's work. A professional portfolio should capture that growth, whether the time span is a semester, a year, or a professional lifetime.

We can say, then, *a professional portfolio is an organized collection of self-selected artifacts and self-generated reflections, developed for a specific purpose and audience that demonstrate the author's professional knowledge, skills, dispositions, and growth over time.*

In this context, an artist's or interior designer's portfolio shown to a potential client in the hope of acquiring a new commission or contract would be a professional portfolio. So, too, would be a teacher's portfolio developed for job-seeking, evaluation, showcase, or professional development purposes be considered a professional portfolio. These types of professional portfolios might contain many of the same artifacts and reflections but would be organized quite differently because they would be targeting different purposes and audiences.

It is important to keep in mind a portfolio should contain each of the defining elements in order to effectively portray the author's professional expertise. A professional portfolio is not difficult to develop, but a truly effective portfolio takes time and thought. A search for professional portfolios on the Internet results in thousands of hits, but a cursory examination of these sites reveals many examples of what a portfolio should not be. Many of these portfolios are ineffective because they lack a clear purpose or audience. Often the organization is poor or does not fit the purpose of the portfolio. Some do not even contain artifacts to document knowledge and skills or growth over time, and many do not include clear, thoughtful reflections. Portfolios such as these are an indication of the popularity of portfolios in the field of education today and the myriad misunderstandings concerning their purpose and development.

Types of Professional Portfolios

Many types of portfolios can be found in literature; for example, references to working portfolios and presentation portfolios are common. These terms identify portfolios by stage of development. This book, however, classifies professional portfolios by purpose and includes the résumé portfolio, the showcase portfolio, the evaluation portfolio, and the professional development portfolio. Because all four are used for various types of evaluation and assessment, they share many characteristics such as the inclusion of reflective pieces and the opportunity for professional growth. The differences among them rest in their purpose, audience, and organization (Figure 1.1). A brief look at each of these portfolios will help clarify their similarities and differences.

Figure 1.1. Types of professional portfolios.

	Purpose	Audience	Organization
Resume Portfolio	To document author's knowledge and skills in order to obtain employment	Department chair School principal Human resources Superintendent	Organized similar to a traditional resume or according to professional standards
Showcase Portfolio	To highlight exceptional work of author to obtain special recognition, such as grant or award	Agency or individual responsible for administration of grant or award	Organized around criteria established by the governing body
Evaluation Portfolio	To portray author's competency to obtain tenure or to meet ongoing evaluation requirements	School principal Human resources superintendent State licensing agency Higher education administrators	Organized around goals, standards, or competencies used for evaluation
Professional Development Portfolio	To document and enhance professional growth	Colleagues Administrators Students Self	Organized around skills, knowledge, dispositions, and evidence of growth, usually of author's choosing

The Résumé Portfolio

The résumé portfolio, as its name implies, is intended to portray a rich and accurate picture of a job seeker to a potential employer. The purpose of a résumé portfolio is to display a wide variety of knowledge and skills to a school principal, department chair, human resources director, and/or superintendent so that the applicant procures a position. With this purpose in mind, the author should organize the portfolio around professional standards or as a traditional résumé would be, with sections for education, previous experience, etc. It should be tailored to fit the specific position for which the applicant is applying. To tailor the résumé in this way might mean inclusion of some artifacts and reflections for one position but not for another. The objective in this instance is to portray knowledge and skills in relation to a specific position so that the applicant is offered the job. The professional résumé portfolio must be organized, structured, and developed with this purpose in mind at all times.

Many education school graduates leave college with portfolios tucked under their arms, a fact that has important implications for veteran teachers in the job market. Even though their portfolios may not strictly be résumé portfolios, these neophytes still have professional portfolios. They are familiar with the portfolio process and probably with the process of reflection. Even though they may not have the classroom experience of a veteran educator, they have experience creating a portfolio, and they will present it to potential employers. Potential employers are likely to expect applicants to present résumé portfolios. As portfolios become more endemic in education programs as requisites for graduation, they are showing up with increasing frequency in interviews. To be without a résumé portfolio in an interview may put the applicant at a decided disadvantage and may even create the impression that she is out-of-date or less than qualified.

The Showcase Portfolio

The showcase portfolio, as the name states, is developed for the purpose of showcasing the author's best work. Depending upon the specific purpose of the showcase portfolio, its scope could be broad or quite narrow. There are a number of instances when a showcase portfolio would be appropriate for a veteran educator: applying for a promotion or tenure; documenting achievement for an award, such as teacher of the year; applying for a grant; or documenting credentials for a consultancy. A preservice teacher may also have need of a showcase portfolio when applying for licensure, grants, scholarships, awards, or assistantships.

The professional showcase portfolio is organized around the knowledge, skills, or attributes required for the goal in question. The organizational components are used as criteria for selecting artifacts from the author's best work.

The Evaluation Portfolio

Today, more than ever, educators are taking an active part in their own evaluation process. For most educators, the days of standardized instruments are gone. Now teachers can often select their own evaluation criteria with goals-based evaluation. Such personalized evaluation allows educators to use portfolios to address evaluation goals in a richer and more thorough way than other types of evaluation documentation allow.

An evaluation portfolio is created by practicing educators and used for ongoing employment evaluation. In some instances, evaluation portfolios are mandated by school or district policy. The distinguishing characteristic of this type of portfolio is that its purpose is to help administrators *examine and judge* the work of a professional employee for the purpose of continued employment or identifying professional strengths and weaknesses. This purpose distinguishes it from the professional development portfolio.

The evaluation portfolio should be organized according to the goals or standards by which the author will be evaluated. In some instances, such as goals-based evaluation, the author is responsible for selecting her own goals. In this situation, professional development is sometimes a component of the evaluation process. In other situations, evaluation focuses on predetermined goals or standards for which the employee must show competence.

The Professional Development Portfolio

Professional development portfolios are created by practicing educators and used to examine specific areas of professional knowledge and skills for the purpose of professional growth. Sometimes, educators themselves decide to author a professional development portfolio. For example, a group of colleagues might decide to develop portfolios as a basis for discussing and evaluating their practices. In other instances, a school or district may require professional development portfolios of its professional staff.

Whether or not the educator has been involved in the portfolio decision, she should have a voice in selecting the professional areas included in the portfolio according to the knowledge base of her field. These areas then become the organizing components of the portfolio. They should also be used as the criteria for selecting artifacts that put the author's skills and knowledge in the best light. During this process, the focus should be on personal assessment by the portfolio's author—determining the contextual importance or value of an artifact—rather than on evaluation or judgment of the author's work by an administrator. The purpose of personal versus external assessment is what distinguishes a professional development portfolio from an evaluation portfolio.

Rationale for Portfolio Development

Professional portfolios are more frequently required by colleges of education as a graduation requirement, by licensing agencies as a certification requirement, and by school districts as a requirement for employment and tenure. Often these agencies rely on performance-based standards similar to those developed by professional organizations, such as the Interstate New Teacher Assessment and Support Consortium (INTASC) and the National Board for Professional Teaching Standards (NBPTS). It is not unreasonable to suggest that in the near future, all practicing educators will be required to develop and maintain some type of evaluation or professional development portfolio.

A primary reason for the growing popularity of professional portfolios is the move toward authentic assessment. Traditional assessment tools, such as standardized tests, do little to inform an employer of a potential employee's effectiveness as an educator. Portfolios, with their variety of artifacts and reflective narratives, provide a unique picture of how the educator functions in an educational context.

A particular advantage of portfolio development is the inclusion of artifacts and reflections is a powerful documentation tool. It is one thing to list accomplishments and competencies on a résumé or grant application; it is quite another to show evidence of those skills and achievements. For example, as a school media specialist you are held accountable for meeting state, district, and national standards in your area. A portfolio not only provides documentation through self-selected artifacts, but the reflections provide thoughtful analysis of your practice and intended growth.

"A professional portfolio . . . can be a convincing, effective vehicle for you to demonstrate to others in a meaningful way the skills and knowledge you have gained in something as complex as teaching" (Cambell, Cignetti, Melenyzer, Nettles, & Wyman, 2001, pp.2-3).

The benefits of developing a professional portfolio are substantial. The résumé portfolio gives a decided edge to a job candidate by presenting a variety of artifacts and reflections that are not possible to include in a traditional résumé. Similarly, the showcase portfolio highlights and contextualizes carefully selected examples of the author's best work. The evaluation portfolio helps administrators judge skills and abilities accurately by presenting them with specific examples, and the professional development portfolio explores the depth and breadth of an educator's practice with an eye toward professional growth.

Portfolios as Evaluation and Assessment Instruments

Professional portfolios have certain important characteristics in common regardless of their purpose. First, the portfolio provides an in-depth look at professional accomplishments most other vehicles merely hint at. Unlike other evaluation and assessment instruments, such as standardized test scores or transcripts, a portfolio is as unique as the author. Although many educators work toward the same professional goals, the different ways those goals are accomplished make each educator unique. A portfolio is a way to showcase an individual's professional personality.

Furthermore, because the design and contents of a portfolio are self-selected, the author has the opportunity to be pro-active by highlighting artifacts that attest to her expertise and growth. This aspect of a portfolio can be especially valuable as a way to enlighten administrators who may not fully appreciate the complexities of particular positions, whether it is that of a media specialist or drama instructor.

The most important benefit of developing a professional portfolio is related to the reflective elements. Without reflection, a collection of professional artifacts is only that—much like my first binder. That collection may very well fit all the other characteristics of a professional portfolio, but reflections are what make it a portfolio. Reflections help give the portfolio the individuality and personality that make it unique. Reflections place each artifact within the context of the author's professional life. They reveal the thoughts, feelings, and attitudes of the author. No other evaluation or assessment instrument provides these insights or is so personal.

Finally, a professional portfolio acts as a record of growth over time. Most of us have had the experience of turning the pages of a photo album that documents the growth of a loved one. We see birthdays, holidays, and personal milestones recorded on the pages from birth to the present. In much the same way, a professional portfolio functions as the documentation of our professional growth. By turning the pages, so to speak, examining the artifacts, and reading the accompanying reflections, we can witness our own professional growth. Again, no other assessment instrument offers such an insightful picture of our careers.

Summary

A professional portfolio is an organized collection of self-selected artifacts and self-generated reflections, developed for a specific purpose and for a specific audience, that demonstrate the author's professional knowledge, skills, attitudes, and growth over time. Many types of portfolios are mentioned in the literature; a common distinction is made between the working portfolio (the portfolio in progress) and the presentation portfolio (the finished portfolio). However, by assuming most professional portfolios are used for some sort of evaluation or assessment, it is helpful to differentiate them by the purpose they serve. In this context, it makes sense to identify the résumé portfolio, the showcase portfolio, the evaluation portfolio, and the professional development portfolio.

Increasingly, portfolios are being required for university graduation, for licensure, for employment, and for evaluation. Standards developed by national organizations such as INTASC and NBPTS are frequently used as organizational elements by many evaluating agencies. Professional portfolios are gaining popularity because they provide an authentic way to evaluate educators. Portfolios provide a unique, in-depth look at an educator's knowledge and skills, practice, beliefs, and attitudes by means of self-selected artifacts and accompanying reflections. In addition, portfolios provide a valuable record of an educator's growth over time for evaluating agencies and for the educator herself.

Chapter Two
Going Digital: Electronic Portfolios

If developing a professional portfolio makes sense, then it makes even more sense to construct it in an electronic format. Electronic portfolios have many advantages over their paper counterparts: they are easier to distribute, can be duplicated quickly and easily, and portray the dynamics of the teaching life more accurately than any traditional portfolio. They do, however, have their limitations: they can be time-consuming, expensive, and stressful, for example. Nevertheless, an electronic portfolio is well worth the investment of time and energy.

What Is an Electronic Portfolio?

Generally speaking, an electronic portfolio can be defined much the same as a traditional portfolio. It, too, is an organized collection of artifacts, selected and reflected upon by the author, and it is developed to fulfill a specific purpose for an intended audience. The difference lies in the format of the artifacts and the methods of portfolio production and presentation. Digital artifacts replace typical paper and three-dimensional ones. Thus, instead of being limited to the confines of a binder, electronic portfolio authors are free to create in a variety of formats, including text, audio, video, graphics, and multimedia. The choice of production tools includes an array of hardware and software. Presentation is also expanded beyond the three-ring notebook to include a variety of storage media and even publication on the World Wide Web.

Benefits of an Electronic Portfolio

Once the decision has been made to develop a portfolio, there are many good reasons to make it electronic. Primary benefits of electronic portfolio development include the following:

• *Much of what educators generate—word documents, slide presentations, Web sites, statistics, and reports— is already in electronic format.* Organizing these various artifacts electronically makes sense. Instead of printing out paper copies, organizing them, preparing them for a binder, and printing reflections, it is much easier to leave the artifacts in digital format, add digital reflections, and organize them electronically. Once the portfolio is created this way, it is easier to maintain, edit, and update than its paper counterpart. Artifacts and reflections can be edited, removed, or rearranged with a few keystrokes instead of the time-consuming tasks of editing, printing, and replacing a binder would require.

- *Much of what educators do does not communicate effectively on the printed page.* Because working with students is dynamic, creative, and stimulating, educators need a vehicle that adequately conveys these characteristics to their portfolio audience. An electronic portfolio that employs a variety of media can present artifacts in ways that convey the vitality of the profession. Text, graphics, audio, and video can be combined in a variety of ways to present a more accurate picture of what transpires in classrooms and media centers, whether it is orienting new students to the media center, storytelling, reenacting a famous historical event, or conducting science experiments. Activities such as these, although typical in the professional lives of educators, can sometimes be difficult to accurately portray within the confines of a standard evaluation instrument or a traditional portfolio.

- *Electronic portfolios can support complex organization for effective documentation.* A major limitation of traditional paper portfolios is they can be organized only in a linear fashion. There is no getting around it—one page must follow another. However, this is not the case with electronic portfolios. Authors can choose a linear organization if that works best, but most often the structure of an electronic portfolio is hierarchical. Through the use of hyperlinks, electronic portfolio developers can organize their portfolios to show relationships between major headings. Supporting artifacts can be linked to more than one heading and

Figure 2.1. Comparison of traditional and electronic portfolio organization

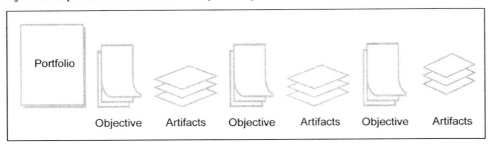

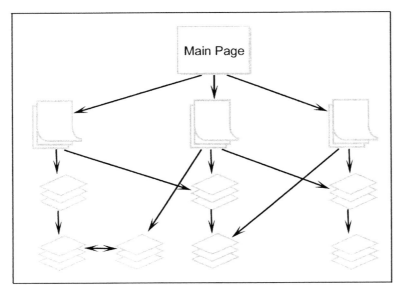

With a traditional portfolio in a notebook or binder, objectives are arranged in order with artifacts directly following. Organization has to be linear.

The most versatile organization for an electronic portfolio is hierarchical, which allows multiple and complex relationships through the use of hyperlinks.

to each other, if necessary, to accurately reflect the complex relationships that exist in our professional practice (Figure 2.1).

- *Electronic portfolios are much easier to reproduce, distribute, and access than their paper counterparts.* A traditional portfolio in a binder is usually limited to one copy, which can be large and unwieldy. Sharing it effectively with more than a few people at a time is difficult. Distributing it to selection committees, prospective employers, or various administrative personnel is prohibitive, not only because of its bulk, but also because of the time and cost involved. In addition, some items, such as original student artwork, projects, and presentation, cannot be satisfactorily reproduced in the traditional paper format.
Electronic portfolios, whether on floppy disk, Zip disk, or CD-ROM, can be easily and quickly reproduced and distributed. Those portfolios published on the Internet can be accessed by a virtual audience at the click of a mouse. This feature is especially important if the portfolio is to be widely distributed. New teachers, for example, can make their portfolios available to multiple prospective employers in advance of an interview instead of bringing their portfolio with them. Similarly, teachers submitting portfolios for board review for a grant, award, tenure, or other achievement can easily supply each member with a copy of their electronic portfolios.

- *Electronic portfolios are an effective way to demonstrate technology skills or learn new ones.* Many educators have come a long way in technology skills development in the last few years. For most, Word documents, PowerPoint presentations, and spreadsheets are an integral part of lesson planning, record keeping, and instruction. These types of programs can all be used effectively to produce an electronic portfolio. For educators who want to expand their technology skills, developing an electronic portfolio is an excellent incentive for doing so. In addition, many states and local school districts are developing or already have in place technology standards for educators. Their purpose is to ensure that educators possess minimum technology proficiencies. Electronic portfolios can be an excellent venue for exhibiting technology proficiency to administrators.

"When published in digital or electronic format, portfolios carry a message of professionalism that can be easily shared with the local and global community and endure over time" (Kilbane & Milman, 2003, xv).

Developing an electronic portfolio is another way to model technology skills for administrators, colleagues, and students. Student portfolios continue to be a popular means of assessment and are used by classroom teachers at all levels. As noted earlier, portfolios are mandatory at many colleges of education, and electronic portfolios are becoming increasingly popular. It makes sense that teachers and instructors should be able to model electronic portfolio development for their students, for other teachers, and for administrators.

- *Electronic portfolios are inexpensive.* If electronic portfolios are created with available software and hardware, then development costs can feasibly be reduced to the price of a few CD-ROMs or other storage medium. True, if the author decides to master new software or needs a scanner, digital camera, or other piece of hardware, then costs can rise so significantly as to be prohibitive, but by using what is already available, an electronic portfolio can be created for pennies (Figure 2.2). In addition, by using hardware and software that have already been mastered, the portfolio developer reduces her learning curve significantly.

Figure 2.2. Cost comparison between traditional and electronic portfolios

Traditional Portfolio		Electronic Portfolio	
Material	Cost	Material	Cost
3" 3-ring binder	7.99	CD-ROM 30@17.98 Jewel case 10@4.99	.60 }$1.10 .50
Paper	3.99	Floppy disk 10@3.99	$ .40
Sheet protectors – 50	9.98	Zip disk – 250 MB 2@14.98	$7.49
Index dividers for laser printer – 5 tab	3.99	Memory key – 128 MB	$69.99

Total Cost - Single	$25.95	Total Cost - Multipack
		   CD-ROM + Jewel case
		   Floppy disk
		   Zip disk
			
			$22.97
			$3.99
			$14.98

The cost of one traditional portfolio, at $25.95, is more than multi-packs of any of the electronic media except for the new memory key. Prices were taken from Office Max and Best Buy Web sites and are subject to change.

Disadvantages of an Electronic Portfolio

If all this sounds to good to be true, and you can't wait to jump on the electronic portfolio bandwagon, then you should first know there are downsides to creating an electronic portfolio. Unfortunately, many books and articles on the subject fail to enumerate the pitfalls that you might encounter. It is important to seriously consider the following issues to make a truly informed decision whether or not to proceed with electronic portfolio development.

- *Electronic portfolio development takes time.* The creation of any professional portfolio, whether traditional or digital, takes time. Portfolios are both a product and a process. If sufficient time and thought is not devoted to the process, the final product will suffer as a result. Careful consideration has to be given to the portfolio's purpose, audience, organization, and format. Reflections must be deep and thorough in order to be effective. The decision to create a portfolio is not one that should be made in haste, and the portfolio itself should not be made that way either. This advice holds true for any portfolio, but you can be sure that developing an electronic portfolio will take substantially more time than a traditional one. In order to develop a portfolio of exceptional quality, you should be sure that you have sufficient time to devote to the process. Surely, at this point, you are wondering, "How much time is enough time?" The answer is, "It depends." It depends upon the level of your technology skills, the complexity of your portfolio's organization, the number of artifacts you choose to include, the thought and care you devote to your reflections, and the necessary technology processes, such as converting artifacts to digital format. Any time something new is thrown into the milieu, such as learning to use new software, the time required for portfolio development increases, sometimes significantly. Time is a valuable commodity to most educators, and there is simply no need to spend yours learning new skills if they are not necessary for portfolio development or not part of your professional development plan. Carefully considering the time you have to devote to electronic portfolio development and then planning accordingly is possibly the most important time you spend on your portfolio.

- *Electronic portfolio development can be expensive.* It is certainly feasible and desirable to create an electronic portfolio with the hardware and software at hand. The benefits of doing so have already been discussed. Nevertheless, there is often a great temptation to use electronic portfolio development as the rationale for buying that really cool digital camera, the latest version of Web authoring software, or both. Beware of such dangerous thinking, which can turn a money-saver into a substantial expense.

- *Electronic portfolio development takes technology skills.* Although it is true that learning new technology skills is not necessary for portfolio development in most cases, the fact still remains that some technology skills are necessary. Portfolios can be created with computing skills so basic that even those who do not know much more than how to open and save a file can create an electronic portfolio. Bells and whistles are not mandatory. However, your level of technology expertise is an important factor in planning and developing your portfolio. If your technology skills are modest, keep your portfolio plan modest as well.

- *Electronic portfolio development can be stressful.* Anyone with any technology experience at all knows, at times, technology can be frustrating, mystifying, and just plain uncooperative ("Why won't it do what I want it to do?"). Times like these lead to stress and then more stress. If you ignore the preceding cautions and allocate insufficient time, buy expensive hardware or software you now must learn how to use, and plan a portfolio far beyond your technological expertise, you might send yourself over the edge. Electronic portfolio development should be a time of professional learning and growing. That is why reflections are the heart of the portfolio. This important truth can easily be overlooked if you have to rush through the process or if you spend most of your time learning new skills. Stress does not lend itself to the clear and careful thinking necessary for organizational and selection decisions, and it surely will detract from any reflective thinking you might attempt.

- *An electronic portfolio might not meet your needs.* In spite of all the sound reasons for electronic portfolio development, authoring one might not be in your best interests in a particular situation. For example, if you are a veteran teacher and decide to complete the application process for national board certification, you can expect to submit a substantial professional portfolio. At this time, however, the requirements specify a paper portfolio and submitting anything else would likely result in it not being scored. It is important, therefore, in any situation, to comply specifically with any instructions or requirements that pertain to your portfolio submission. Another reason you might decide against an electronic portfolio involves the technological expertise of your audience. If possible, you should match the technological sophistication of the portfolio with the expertise of the portfolio's audience. If you are not acquainted with your audience, then it would be best to err on the side of caution and submit a portfolio that involves few technology skills to open and view.

The Technology Factor

By now you have several aspects of electronic portfolio development to consider as you decide whether proceeding to the planning phase is right for you. Before you make that decision, one more discussion of the technology factor is in order. This one centers on the issue of priorities.

It is important to keep in mind the number-one priority of portfolio development is content. Whether electronic or paper, a flashy presentation cannot redeem a portfolio that is poorly designed, carelessly constructed, and lacking in authentic reflection. However, even the best portfolio can be undermined by a flawed presentation. Herein lies the crux of the issue: finding and keeping a desirable balance between portfolio content and portfolio technology.

Yes, the technological skills you employ in constructing your portfolio speak to your level of expertise. Since technology is an increasingly necessary skill for educators to possess, it is desirable to present a portfolio that displays your technology skills in the best possible light. Displaying one's technological expertise is one of the benefits of electronic portfolio development. However, these skills should never overshadow the content of the portfolio.

This situation can easily occur if you are learning new technology or if you are a technology whiz. In the first instance, as previously noted, you can expend far too much time and attention on mastering new hardware or software. Since there is presumably a limit to the amount of time you can devote to your portfolio, some other aspect of your portfolio is neglected. Unfortunately, that aspect is often the reflective elements, artifact selection, or some other critical element of portfolio content. If you are a technological wizard, you might be tempted to pull out all the stops and make your portfolio so flashy the technology overpowers the content. Even though your artifacts are excellent and your reflections truly insightful, they might become lost in all the glitz.

Hence, the need for balance between portfolio content and portfolio technology. **Content is always more important than the technology used to create it.** Remember, technology, as marvelous or aggravating as it can be, is merely a tool, a means to an end. The process of portfolio development, complete with reflections, should lead to professional growth as an educator. Focusing on portfolio content will allow that process to happen.

Summary

An electronic portfolio meets the defining criteria of its paper counterpart. However, it has several benefits a paper portfolio does not: In addition to being an effective method of demonstrating your technology skills, an electronic portfolio takes advantage of the fact that much of an educator's materials are already in electronic format and are therefore easier to assemble, organize, edit, delete, or rearrange. By taking advantage of audio, video, and graphic media, you can accurately and dynamically convey your practice in a way paper cannot accomplish. Furthermore, various elements of your practice can be linked to each other or to standards and goals in a much more complex fashion than is possible in a binder. Finally, electronic portfolios can be created, reproduced, and distributed quite inexpensively if you stick to the software and hardware you already have.

Electronic portfolio development has some disadvantages associated with it as well. For example, the process takes a lot of time and can be very stressful, especially if you have decided to master new hardware or software in the course of portfolio development. In that case, an electronic portfolio could prove to be quite expensive. You might also discover the new skills are more than you can handle during the portfolio process or you have designed a portfolio too ambitious for the skills you currently possess. Finally, an electronic portfolio might not meet your needs or the requirements of your audience. However, if you do decide to proceed with an electronic portfolio, remember content is always more important than technology. If you ignore this tenet, then you have missed the point.

Chapter Three
Portfolio Development Considerations

Once you have made the decision to develop a professional portfolio, you may be eager to begin creating it right away. Although enthusiasm for the task will do much to help you along the way, it is a good idea to spend some quality time planning the portfolio before you begin developing it. Planning will help you proceed in an orderly and efficient manner, reducing or eliminating many false starts, and will help you avoid faulty decisions, reorganizing, and other pitfalls that can occur along the way.

Let's start by referring to the definition of a professional portfolio again and by paying particular attention to the three areas of focus: *A professional portfolio is an organized collection of self-selected artifacts and self-generated reflections, developed for a **specific purpose** and **audience**, that demonstrate the author's **professional knowledge, skills, dispositions, and growth** over time.*

By thinking about these basic considerations of portfolio development prior to beginning the actual portfolio, you will be utilizing the very tool that will make your portfolio uniquely yours—the tool of reflection. Reflection will ensure that you properly and specifically identify and define the development considerations that are crucial to portfolio success. A look at these considerations will illustrate how they impact successful portfolio development and how they are implemented in each type of professional portfolio.

Identifying Your Purpose

A professional portfolio is developed to accomplish a particular purpose, just like a piece of effective writing. In order for your portfolio to be effective, then, you first need to decide on the portfolio's purpose. The portfolio's purpose might be to serve as a résumé, an evaluation instrument, a professional showcase, or a professional development piece. Whatever the portfolio's function will be, that purpose should be identified first before anything else is accomplished.

Determining what function the portfolio will perform is important to accomplish first because the portfolio's purpose is the decisive factor in

"A clear sense of purpose will help you put forward a consistent effort toward creating a successful Web portfolio. . . . Writing down your purposes explicitly will help you set priorities, make goals, and determine the tone, appearance, and contents of your portfolio" (Kimball, 2003, p. 45).

determining its goals, objectives, and organization. If the portfolio will function as a résumé, for example, it will have different goals, objectives, and organization than an evaluation portfolio. Similarly, a showcase portfolio would be unlike a professional development portfolio. Different purposes require unique organization in order to achieve different goals and objectives.

If you think you might need more than one type of portfolio (for example, you may need one for evaluation and another to serve as a showcase), it is tempting to consider developing a generic portfolio that could serve as a "one-size-fits-all" instrument. However, it is better by far to invest the extra time to create different portfolios that target different, specific purposes. Even though you may incorporate several of the same artifacts within both portfolios, different organization will go a long way toward accomplishing the different purposes you hope to achieve. Chances are, most of us will need different types of portfolios during the course of our careers. Understanding the differences in terms of purpose, goals and objectives, and audience can help us select and develop the right portfolio to fit our needs.

The Résumé Portfolio

All beginning teachers will want to have a résumé portfolio as they venture out into the job market, and veteran educators who are looking for a new position will find themselves in need of an effective résumé portfolio as well. If your portfolio will function as your résumé, then your purpose will be to secure a professional position. You may be seeking a position as an English teacher, media specialist, guidance counselor, or assistant principal—regardless of the position, a résumé portfolio can help. Similarly, whether you are seeking initial employment, applying for a promotion, or changing positions, a well-made résumé portfolio can highlight your education, training, and previous experience that qualify you for the job.

If you are currently a student or have recently graduated from a teacher education program, it is likely you have already developed a portfolio. Your portfolio is probably organized around professional teaching standards and the experience you gained in each during your teacher training. For the purpose of finding initial employment, this portfolio may work well for you, particularly if your artifacts are well chosen and if your reflections are insightful and clearly written. The next step is to consider making your portfolio electronic if it isn't already, and to look at ways you can make your résumé portfolio more specific to the position you are seeking.

A well-developed and specific purpose is essential at this point. Your purpose needs to be more focused than merely "looking for a position in elementary education." The important consideration here is to be specific. What particular position do you want? Are you looking for a job in upper elementary? Do you want a position in a particular school district? If you can target the type of position you want, then you can make your portfolio fit that job as closely as possible. The better the fit, the better your chances of finding and getting the job you want.

If you want to get a job as a middle school science teacher, for example, then that should be the purpose of your portfolio, and every consequent decision you make about your portfolio should be qualified by that purpose. If you are willing to change locations, are qualified to teach in more than one content area, or are otherwise flexible in your job search, then you may need to retarget your portfolio for each different position for which you apply. You may have your heart set on teaching middle school language arts, but the only opening in your locale is in high school English. In order for your middle school portfolio to fulfill its new purpose of getting a high school English job, you will have to review your portfolio and tweak it so it displays your experience and accomplishments in the best possible light for that high school position.

Specifically defining your purpose will help you immensely as you plan and develop your professional portfolio. Narrowing the lens by which you view all your experience, accomplishments, and training will help you focus on the specific events in your professional history that will be most helpful in achieving your purpose. You will find this approach is especially helpful as you gain more experience and collect more artifacts from which to choose. With a specific purpose, you can easily identify the significant artifacts your résumé should highlight.

The Showcase Portfolio

A showcase portfolio is similar to a résumé portfolio in that you are using it to try to obtain something, but instead of a job you are trying for funding, recognition, or an honor of some kind. Typically, a showcase portfolio is developed for a "special occasion." Maybe you are applying for a grant or are competing for an award such as teacher of the year for your district or state. Whatever the reason, developing a showcase portfolio is precipitated by an event that is usually one time only and quite specific.

This makes it easy to identify the purpose for your portfolio. If, for example, you are developing a portfolio as part of a grant application for science lab equipment, then your purpose might be "to develop a showcase portfolio that illustrates my ability to implement a science lab in my sixth grade science class." Maybe you are looking for funding for computers for the media center. Then your purpose might be, "to develop a showcase portfolio that highlights my qualifications to initiate and develop a technology skills program for the media center." Maybe you are developing a showcase portfolio to apply for teacher of the year. Then your purpose might be, "to develop a showcase portfolio that highlights my accomplishments and best practice teaching third grade last year."

Whatever the occasion for developing your showcase portfolio, it will help you begin to focus if you identify the portfolio's purpose as a first step. You may think the purpose is so obvious it is unnecessary to commit it to paper. However, once you begin to think about your purpose and to consider it carefully, you will find that writing it down will help you articulate exactly what you need to accomplish.

The Evaluation Portfolio

Annual job performance evaluation is a fact of life in the teaching profession. Whether you are a first-year novice or a thirty-year veteran, you will probably be observed and evaluated at least once during the school year. If you are beginning your career, chances are you will experience several evaluations during the year. Some will take the form of observations, others might be critiques of lesson plans, and still others might be conferences with principals or other administrators. Some evaluations will be structured while others might be more informal. Whatever the occasion or format, evaluations are a part of a teacher's professional life.

Portfolios, both traditional and electronic, are becoming increasingly popular as evaluation instruments. In some states and local districts, portfolios are becoming popular, not only for evaluation, but also for initial licensure. Anyone who has applied for certification from the National Board of Professional Teaching Standards (NBPTS) knows portfolio development is an integral part of evaluation process.

Portfolio development is a way for teachers to participate more actively in their own evaluation process. By developing an evaluation portfolio, it is possible to explore aspects of your practice that might not receive as much attention as you would like with strictly traditional evaluation methods. For example, you may note that you weeded three hundred books from your media center's collection last year. That fairly boring fact could take on new significance if it were illustrated by a picture of you with that mountain of books. The reflective elements give you a more active voice in your evaluation as well. Even if you are not required to submit an evaluation portfolio, developing one will help you and your evaluator explore your practice more thoroughly.

As with other portfolios, it is important to carefully determine the specific purpose of your evaluation portfolio before development begins. If you are a first or second-year teacher, for example, then your purpose might be "to develop an evaluation portfolio that displays the competencies required for tenure." If you are already a tenured teacher, then your purpose might focus on a particular competency, such as: "to develop a portfolio that evaluates my use of technology in the classroom."

In some cases, you may have a say in the areas in which you are evaluated. In other instances, you may not. Either way, using the evaluation criteria to craft your portfolio's purpose begins the process of focusing your portfolio for maximum effect.

The Professional Development Portfolio

It could be said every portfolio is a professional development portfolio in the sense that its creation helps the author focus and reflect upon her teaching. Although that statement is certainly true, the portfolio that is developed for the purpose of professional development exhibits its own characteristics.

Like the evaluation portfolio, a professional development portfolio is developed to help practicing teachers look at the work they do with a critical eye. However, a professional development portfolio usually is initiated by its author as a self-selected professional development activity versus being a mandate of the district, state, or other governing body. Unlike an evaluation portfolio that focuses exclusively on best work, a professional development portfolio often looks at career components that the author would like to improve or develop.

Like evaluation portfolios, a professional development portfolio gives its creator an active voice. The author speaks to her professional development, not only through the facets of her practice she chooses to explore, but also through her reflections. What distinguishes the professional development portfolio from the others is its emphasis on what has been learned from past experiences and how that knowledge will affect future practice.

The purpose of a professional development portfolio, then, is reflection that will lead to professional growth. This is not to say a professional development portfolio must focus on weaknesses or faults. On the contrary, your professional development portfolio may target knowledge or skills you already have, but the key is to focus on improvement. Because a professional development portfolio is used to direct the future path of your career, it is important you carefully consider the areas you want to target for growth. These areas will become the purpose of your portfolio.

Let's say you have been in the classroom for several years; your students think your class is boring, and frankly, you're bored too. Maybe, your portfolio's purpose would be "to develop a portfolio that explores and evaluates my teaching methodologies." On the surface, the purpose of this portfolio looks as if it could also serve quite well as an evaluation portfolio. However, the author of the professional development portfolio knows the knowledge and analysis that she procures will lead to specific plans for future growth.

Maybe, you are in awe of your colleagues who can engage their students with PowerPoint presentations and WebQuests, while it is all you can do to answer your e-mail. You may want to create a professional development portfolio that has as its purpose "to examine my computer skills and how I use technology in the classroom." The focus is on an aspect of your career you would like to develop or improve. The professional development portfolio can help you get there.

Possibly, you have always received excellent evaluations from your principal, but lately you've been wondering what you can do to grow professionally. It could be time to look at your practice with an eye toward professional development. Your purpose might be "to identify three areas in my professional practice where I can grow and improve."

In each case, it is true that you are evaluating your practice, but the emphasis is always on future growth and personal satisfaction with the path of your career. Of all the professional portfolios, the professional development portfolio is the most personal, the most reflective, and possibly the most fulfilling.

Portfolio Goals and Objectives

Once you have identified the purpose of your portfolio, developing its goal will come easily. In fact, you may have already realized that identifying your purpose is tantamount to defining your portfolio's goal. If, for example, you have decided to develop a portfolio for the purpose of obtaining employment as a high school media specialist, your goal is to document your *knowledge, skills, dispositions, and growth* that qualify you for the particular position of high school media specialist. Your portfolio's purpose, then, is its reason for being, and your goal is a statement of what you will demonstrate to achieve that purpose.

After identifying and articulating your purpose and goal, your objectives will help you get your portfolio where it needs to go. Portfolio objectives work like good lesson plan objectives; they serve as the means to the end. If you learned to write objectives by prefacing them with the phrase, "The student will be able to . . . ," then this familiar strategy will serve you well in portfolio development. Start your portfolio objectives by adapting that phrase to say, "My portfolio will demonstrate that . . ."

Deciding what follows is a critical step in portfolio development. Just like a lesson that can succeed or fail on the basis of teaching objectives, a portfolio can also succeed or fail on the basis of its objectives. What should your objectives say that your portfolio will demonstrate? The definition of a portfolio tells us that objectives need to address *knowledge, skills, dispositions, and growth* as they relate to the goal of the portfolio. How, then, do you decide what your portfolio objectives will be, and how do you decide what knowledge, skills, dispositions, and growth will exemplify those objectives?

There are several sources to help you make that decision. First, you should carefully consider the content of the document that initiated your portfolio development. If you are developing a résumé portfolio, study the vacancy notice to determine what particular competencies are being sought. Similarly, if you are developing a showcase or evaluation portfolio, it is likely that there are standards, guidelines, or requirements that will help you in determining the objectives of your portfolio. Look for the types of knowledge, skills, dispositions, and growth specifically mentioned in the vacancy notice, application guidelines, or evaluation criteria to help determine what your objectives should be.

Another source to consider is the appropriate professional standards for your field or content area. Review the competencies professionals in your field are expected to have. If you are a member of the professional organization for your content area, then you are already aware of or have access to this information through professional journals, membership materials, or Web sites. Consider professional standards carefully as you determine the objectives of your portfolio.

Additional resources may be available from your state department of education and your local school district. Some state agencies have developed competencies and instructional standards that can help you specify your portfolio objectives. Similarly, your district may have professional development materials that can help you formulate thoughtful and well-crafted objectives for your portfolio, whatever its purpose and goal (Figure 3.1).

Let's look at a job-seeking media specialist to see how she might develop her objectives. In response to the following notice:

MEDIA SPECIALIST Vacancy. Position requires ability to work closely with classroom teachers and oversee computer lab. Must have excellent managerial and communication skills. Will work with parent volunteers and supervise student helpers. Media center operates on flexible schedule. Experience preferred. Apply to Sunnyview Heights Middle School.

Figure 3.1. Conceptual development of a professional portfolio.

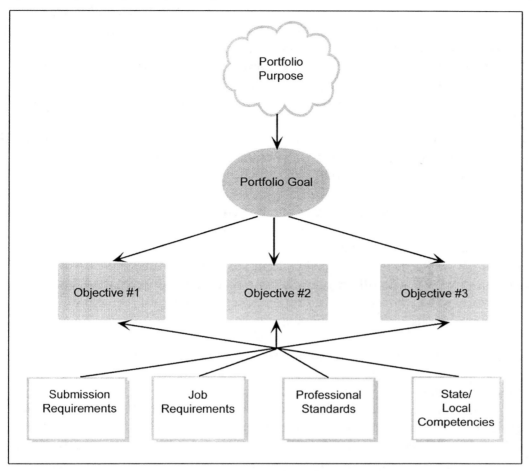

A professional portfolio is developed from a purpose and the resulting goal. Objectives that support the goal are derived from portfolio requirements, professional standards, and other relevant standards, competencies, and requirements.

Our media specialist first needs to identify the requirements specified in the vacancy notice and align them with professional standards (Appendix A). Ideally, job requirements will align closely with professional standards, but they may not always be a perfect fit. In her case, not all professional standards were listed in the vacancy notice. However, when a job requirement is also a professional standard, she must make sure to target this area in her objectives. She further decides that managerial skills include the ability to work with student helpers and volunteers and that she could display her communication skills through her portfolio and subsequent interview. After careful consideration, she chooses on the following objectives:

- *My portfolio will demonstrate that* I have the knowledge and skills to manage all aspects of a media program.
- *My portfolio will demonstrate that* I am a willing and enthusiastic collaborative partner with classroom teachers.
- *My portfolio will demonstrate that* I have the skills and experience to operate and maintain a successful technology program.

These areas are important to the field of librarianship and are addressed directly in the vacancy notice. It is critical these areas be addressed directly by our media specialist's objectives. Such decisions should not be made hastily; without proper consideration of her objectives, her portfolio may not meet its goal, and consequently, not achieve its purpose.

If you are developing a showcase or evaluation portfolio, the areas in which you demonstrate your proficiency may be chosen for you. For example, let's imagine you are developing an evaluation portfolio, and the evaluation instrument requires you demonstrate proficiency in instruction, collaboration, and integration of technology. In this case, you might want your objectives to be:

- *My portfolio will demonstrate that* I am knowledgeable of and employ a variety of instructional methodologies in my teaching repertoire to provide meaningful learning activities for all students.
- *My portfolio will demonstrate that* I collaborate with my colleagues, both within my department and with others in my school, district, state, and nation.
- *My portfolio will demonstrate that* I integrate technology into preparation, instruction, and classroom management.

If your portfolio is a professional development piece, then the objectives you select are probably your decision. Just remember to align them to your portfolio's goal and your purpose of professional growth.

No matter what type of portfolio you are developing, make sure you do two things: first, identify any and all requirements pertaining to the portfolio's content; second, target the content requirements in your goal and objectives. These two steps will help ensure you identify the correct artifacts and documentation to include in your portfolio and organize them in such a way as to clearly fulfill submission requirements.

It is important to note this is not the step at which you select artifacts to include in your portfolio. If you are like most people, you probably have already generated a list (either on paper or at least in your head) of specific pieces you think you want to include in the finished portfolio. Maybe you are thinking of an exceptionally good classroom observation you had last year, or a letter of appreciation you received from the superintendent, or maybe that PowerPoint you developed to teach frog dissection. Although this is tempting, you are not there yet. Try to refrain from working on this list as much as possible at this point.

Portfolio Organization

The organization of your portfolio is usually determined by its purpose and tied closely to its goals and objectives. Organization is an important aspect of portfolio development and should be carefully considered before development begins. Whether paper or electronic, your portfolio should be arranged in a way that is logical, easily accessible, appropriate for the purpose of your portfolio, and suited to your audience. The organization of your portfolio should highlight its contents yet be unobtrusive to the user. Organizational decisions can be challenging, but taking the time to make good ones will be well worth the time and planning they take. Remember to keep your portfolio's purpose clearly in mind as you decide how to organize your material.

Another consideration in planning your portfolio's organization is its electronic format. With a traditional portfolio, organization is linear. You have to decide what your major headings will be and in what order to place them, but ultimately they are put in a binder, one after another. Although you can create an electronic portfolio that has a linear organization, the inclusion of hyperlinks gives you the ability to link objectives, artifacts, documentation, and reflections in a myriad of arrangements. You will need to thoughtfully determine which associations are the most meaningful in order to keep your portfolio's organization logical, clear, and easy to use.

If you are developing a résumé portfolio, you may want to use an organizational structure similar to a traditional résumé with sections for Education, Experience, Accomplishments, and so forth. However, if you are a beginning teacher or are changing fields, this format might not suit you best. It might be to your benefit to organize your materials according to the INTASC standards for new teachers. Revisit the purpose of your portfolio and reread your goal and objectives. Then decide what format will help you present your materials in the best light to accomplish your goal and achieve your purpose. In the end, there is no one right way for everyone; only you can decide how to best organize your portfolio.

If you are developing a showcase portfolio or an evaluation portfolio, then possibly the organizing elements of your portfolio have been determined for you as part of submission requirements. In this situation, you would have to follow the format specified for submission, but before beginning, you would still identify your goal and objectives so your portfolio targets those areas that clearly pertain to submission requirements. The requirements of the evaluation instrument can give you the particular skills or competencies you will identify, first in your objectives and later in portfolio development. Then, you can turn to national, state, and local professional standards for help in deciding the specific areas to target in your objectives.

Even if submission and content requirements determine the purpose, goal, and objectives of your portfolio, you will still need to consider these elements as you make your organizational decisions. Doing so will make your portfolio more effective in terms of addressing its purpose. This chapter began by comparing portfolio development to writing with a purpose. Return to the writing analogy and compare your portfolio's goal to a good thesis statement and your objectives to the topics identified in that statement. Just like a good thesis statement, the portfolio's goal and objectives provide the structure, form, and content of what is to come.

If the writing analogy makes you squirm, then consider the lesson plan analogy instead. Your portfolio goal is equivalent to your lesson goal. Each objective in your lesson, as you know, must support the goal of the lesson. Similarly, each objective in your portfolio must support the goal of your portfolio. The same strategy that produces a strong lesson can also develop a strong, targeted portfolio, a portfolio that accomplishes its purpose.

Who Is Your Audience?

Finally, you need to consider who your portfolio's audience will be before you begin the development process. This consideration is important because it affects not only the content of your portfolio, but also the format of your portfolio and the tools you will use to create it. Because your portfolio will be electronic, you will want to pay particular attention to your potential audience. A portfolio developed without careful consideration of your audience can tarnish your professional image; carefully considering your audience in portfolio development can make you shine. Your goal is to create a portfolio that is user-friendly to everyone who accesses it. At this point, then, we need to consider not just content, but also production.

The first issue to address is format. Typically, submission requirements do not specify if an electronic portfolio is acceptable. You will definitely want to ascertain that it is before you begin development. Although educators are becoming increasingly receptive to the concept of electronic portfolios, you do not want to submit an electronic document to someone who is disinclined to appreciate one. If you know the person or persons who will review your portfolio (your principal, for example), you may already know if an electronic portfolio is acceptable. Otherwise, you may need to ask.

After you are assured that an electronic portfolio is appropriate, then you must consider the level of technological expertise of your audience. If you are submitting a résumé portfolio, for example, you will most likely be submitting it to a human resources director you do not know. Possibly, one or more building principals will be reviewing your submission. Maybe the district superintendent and a department chair will have a look as well. If you are submitting a showcase portfolio for a local, state, or national grant or award, you may not have any idea how the review process functions or who will look at your submission. If this is your situation, how can you be sure your portfolio is accessible to everyone who may be part of its audience?

The answer is to adapt a tactic commonly employed by the publishing industry. Publishers of popular newspapers and magazines know to write to the average national reading level or lower. Doing so, ensures that their publications are accessible to the majority of potential readers in their market. A similar strategy can also work for you, as you think about developing your portfolio. Think of your portfolio in terms of the software and technology you might use to create it, and then think of your potential audience and what you know—or don't know—about their technological savvy. Make sure that the programs you incorporate into the production of your portfolio are readily accessible to your potential audience. They should be user-friendly, even for a computer novice.

You might be a technological wonder and be able to create a portfolio with dazzling graphics, awesome audio, and stunning video. However, if the human resources director can barely open his e-mail, your portfolio may not be appreciated or even accessible to the one person whose perusal is most critical. It is entirely possible to "portfolio" yourself out of a job, scholarship, award, or evaluation just because you do not know your audience or fail to consider their prowess with a computer.

Know your audience, know their predisposition to electronic submissions, and if you can, get a sense of their computer competence. If you are not sure or do not know what they know, play it safe and keep your development plans simple. Sometimes less is more.

Summary

Planning your portfolio before you begin development will go a long way toward helping you avoid various pitfalls, setbacks, and frustrations. Additionally, planning will give you a clear focus of where you are going, why you are headed there, and how you will get there. Think of planning as mapping the route to the destination you want to achieve. In order to arrive at your intended destination, you will need to identify your purpose, identify your goal and objectives, and know your audience.

Identifying your purpose means you have a specific task for your portfolio to fulfill. Generally, your portfolio's purpose might be to function as a résumé, a showcase, an evaluation instrument, or a professional development piece. However, your purpose should be as specific as possible to provide a tight focus for portfolio development.

Once you have a specific purpose, the next step is to develop a goal for your portfolio. If the portfolio's purpose can be conceived of as the reason why you are developing a portfolio, then the goal states what your portfolio will accomplish. Let's create a hypothetical situation. A vacancy for an art teacher was recently advertised, and you want to apply. You decide to develop a résumé portfolio to help you secure the position; that is your purpose. What your portfolio will do—display the knowledge, skills, dispositions, and growth that qualify you for the vacancy at East End Middle School—is your portfolio's goal.

Next come objectives. They complete the sentence, "My portfolio will demonstrate that . . ." It is important to select objectives carefully for several reasons. As you formulate your objectives, you determine the specific knowledge, skills, dispositions, and areas of growth that you want to highlight in your portfolio. You must make sure that you account for all requirements specified in the vacancy notice or submission requirements. You also want to make sure you consider and include appropriate professional standards. Once you have chosen specific areas to target, it will be easier to select artifacts and documentation for your portfolio contents. Good objectives help you determine the content of your portfolio—content that will help your portfolio achieve its goal. Well-written objectives are the bridge that connects content with your goal.

Once you have a purpose, goal, and objectives, you should begin thinking about how your portfolio will be organized. Good organization ensures your contents are easily accessible. Good organization helps make sense of your content and is appropriate for your purpose. Organizational considerations can be challenging, especially in an electronic format. Since you are not confined to a linear arrangement, it is more important than ever to think about relationships between objectives and individual artifacts. It is also important to make sure you consider any submission requirements that you need to meet.

Your final consideration before you begin developing your portfolio is your potential audience. It is important to know who your audience will be, their position on portfolios in general and electronic portfolios in particular, and their level of computer expertise. If you are submitting an evaluation portfolio to your principal, this information will be easily ascertained. In other instances, you may not know much about your audience at all. If this is the position in which you find yourself, make very sure your portfolio is easily accessible, arranged logically, and user-friendly. Use software programs that are readily available and that operate seamlessly. It is better to submit a simple portfolio is rich in content than a technologically sophisticated portfolio that cannot be accessed.

Chapter Four
Portfolio Development: What did I do?

You have come a long way since you started this book, even though you have not, as yet, started to develop your portfolio. You know what a professional portfolio is and why you need one. You have made the decision to develop an electronic portfolio. You have identified the purpose of your portfolio and have formulated its goal and objectives. Now it is time to begin developing the contents of your portfolio.

As we begin, we need to take a moment to look ahead at the conceptual process you will use to develop your portfolio. The literature contains a number of methods of portfolio development, but it really asks three questions: "What did I do?" "What did I learn?" and "What will I do next?" These three questions, developed by Van Wagenen and Hibbard (1998), capture the essence of portfolio development. Another helpful approach is to look at the big picture using Helen Barrett's (2000b) four steps for portfolio development. These two models (Figure 4.1) help to remind us that the focus of portfolio development, whether traditional or electronic, is on professional knowledge, skills, dispositions, and growth. The focus of the portfolio must remain its contents. The technology employed to create it is important but always secondary.

Figure 4.1. Comparison of two approaches to portfolio development.

	Four Processes for Portfolio Development	Three Questions for Portfolio Development
Content {	Collection Selection	What did I do?
	Reflection	What did I learn?
	Projection	What will I do next?
Technology	Presentation and Production	

The four-step process of collection, selection, reflection, and projection was modified from Barrett's Electronic portfolio development (2000b). Van Wagenen & Hibbard's questions appear in Building Teacher Portfolios (1998).

Now that you know where your portfolio is going, take a moment to revisit where you have been. Go back and reread your purpose, goal, and objectives. You may have them memorized by now, but it is important to stay focused on what you are trying to accomplish and why you are doing it. Then, in light of what you have just read, think about the question: "What did I do?"

Actually, you will answer a more specific question: "What did I do that pertains to one or more of my portfolio objectives?" By focusing only on accomplishments that pertain to your objectives, you are performing an initial screening process that will help you focus on only those items that should actually be considered for inclusion in the portfolio. It is also important to make sure nothing relevant gets discarded. At this point, make sure you collect anything and everything that might possibly have a place in your final portfolio while eliminating those items that definitely do not belong.

The Working Portfolio

What you are doing at this stage is creating your working portfolio. Some portfolio developers would argue there are really only two types of portfolios: working portfolios and finished portfolios, and from a production perspective, they are right. However, in the sense that your portfolio is a record of your professional life, the portfolio is never finished until you are—retired, that is. Your portfolio, like your career, is always a work in progress. Creating your working portfolio, then, is a process that can continue throughout your career. The first task is to identify any and all artifacts that might possibly pertain to the focus of your portfolio. Then you will select those artifacts that you want to include in the finished portfolio, and begin the process of organizing them effectively.

Identifying Artifacts

To begin developing your portfolio, you first need to collect artifacts. In portfolio construction an artifact is an item or piece of evidence that helps document professional expertise. An artifact can be anything from an assessment instrument to a seating plan as long as it helps to document and demonstrate your work toward a specific objective.

The authors of *How to Develop a Professional Portfolio: A Manual for Teachers* have developed an Artifact Checklist that has been modified to fit our portfolio development needs (Campbell, Cignetti, Melenyzer, Nettles, & Wyman, 2001). You can use this listing to spark your thinking about your own particular artifacts (Appendix B). Do not feel constrained by the items on the list; neither should you feel compelled to provide all of the artifacts listed. Some items are more suitable for beginning teachers or new graduates, while other items will be more appropriate for veteran educators.

The listing of artifacts is designed so you can check or number each artifact (for organizational purposes) you have selected and identify which of your objectives it meets. This listing will help tremendously as you begin organizing your artifacts for your portfolio construction. You will be able to easily see where your evidence is strongest and which objective may need more substantiation. The list will also help you identify the different types of artifacts you have collected: do you really want all of your artifacts to be lesson plans, or are there other items you could use?

Carefully consider your objectives as you reflect upon all the possible types of evidence of your practice. Chances are, if you take your time and comb through your file cabinets, lesson plans, and computer files, you will find a surprising array of artifacts that pertain to one or more of the objectives you have targeted for your portfolio. You will find evidence of activities and events you may have forgotten. Review school calendars and newsletters and you may find even more evidence to include in your portfolio. Talk to colleagues and administrators for additional ideas.

Working through the collection phase of portfolio development does more than help you identify artifacts to consider for your portfolio. In addition, it helps you develop a new perspective on your career. It is easy to become short-sighted because of the daily demands of the job; collecting artifacts for your portfolio helps you to step back and take a look at all you have done. It can be a very gratifying experience to realize that all of those little things really do add up. Collection can help you realize "all those little things" are not really so little after all. When you think about your activities in light of professional objectives, you can readily see how relevant each of your activities is, even though they may not seem so in the hubbub of the average school day.

Collecting evidence of your professional practice should lead you to an interesting array of materials. You may have video tapes of your concert choir or trophies from your debate team, handicraft projects made by you or your students, newsletters, personal teaching journals—the possibilities are as varied as your teaching practices.

Now, you may wonder, how can you possibly include all of this "stuff" in your portfolio? That query has two responses. The first addresses the number of artifacts. Remember, this is your working portfolio. This means every artifact which pertains to your objectives has the possibility of inclusion in the final product, but not all of them *will* be included in your finished portfolio. Your mission, at this point, is to collect as many artifacts as possible. If in doubt whether a particular artifact is suitable, err on the side of excess and include it. It is much easier to discard it at a later date than to rummage through your files later, muttering, "I know I saw it in here somewhere."

This brings us to the second response. At this phase of portfolio development, you should only be collecting, not spending time scanning paper documents, taking photographs, or recording videos. Remember, not all artifacts will make the final cut so don't worry about getting all of your artifacts into an electronic format right now. You will not be using all of these artifacts, so digitizing all of them at this point would be a tremendous drain on your portfolio development time. Getting your artifacts into electronic format will come later.

Selecting Artifacts

Once you are satisfied you have collected all artifacts that pertain to your portfolio's objectives, it is time to move on to the next step. You have answered the question, "What did I do that pertains to one or more of my portfolio objectives?" Now you must answer a more specific question, "What did I do best?" To do this, you will examine each of your artifacts in light of the objective it was selected to document.

If you used the Artifact Checklist, then you can begin to examine each of your artifacts in a systematic way. If you have a relatively small number of artifacts, it may be easy for you to complete the selection process in one step: yes or no, it's in or it's out. However, if you have a large number of artifacts, you may need to cull them more than once as you consider and then reconsider each piece's value to the final portfolio.

As you work your way through the selection process, you will examine each artifact from multiple perspectives. There are several characteristics that an artifact may possess that would make it a strong candidate for your portfolio.

- *Does the artifact strongly support one or more portfolio objectives?* The artifacts that meet this criterion should be at the top of your selection list. When compiling a portfolio for National Board Certification, you are advised to submit evidence that is consistent, clear, and convincing. That recommendation works well for other professional portfolios as well.
- *Examine the artifact in light of professional standards.* This strategy is closely aligned to the first. Identifying pertinent standards relating those standards to particular artifacts can help you make choices that strongly support professional expectations.
- *Which artifacts represent your best work?* It is critical that your portfolio contains evidence of best practice. Even if you are demonstrating growth, you will compare earlier best practice to current pedagogy. Select those artifacts that highlight your strengths.

The artifacts that meet any of these criteria should remain in the running; those artifacts that meet all three criteria should definitely be included in your portfolio.

Once you have selected artifacts using these first three criteria, you will have a large collection that you should further refine.

- *Consider the number of artifacts for each objective.* Although you do not need to have a equal number of artifacts for each objective, you should be aware of the balance among the objectives in your portfolio. You also want to make sure that you completely support each objective with appropriate artifacts.
- *Look at the types of artifacts you have selected.* Try to include a variety of artifacts so that your audience can see that you are capable of meeting your objectives in a variety of ways.
- *Consider the formats of your artifacts.* You have collected multiple artifacts, and you also want a collection of multiple formats. No matter how good each of them is, you do not want your portfolio to include only PowerPoint presentations, . A variety of formats not only keeps your portfolio interesting, but also displays your expertise in a variety of venues.

If you have carefully developed your portfolio's goal and objectives and have thoughtfully considered your artifacts in light of the recommended selection process, then you are ready to consider how many artifacts to include in your portfolio. How many artifacts do you need? Again, it depends. Sometimes the criteria for your portfolio may be specific, and you will know exactly what you need to submit. Many other times, however, you will have to rely on your own judgment to know that you have selected and included the documentation to meet your portfolio's goal.

> "A portfolio is a sampling of the breadth and depth of a person's work conveying the range of abilities, attitudes, experiences, and achievements" (Lamb, 2002).

Now it is a good idea to review each objective and make sure that your selected artifacts document every facet of the objective. Make sure your documentation is sufficient without being repetitive. You want enough pieces to provide complete documentation, but not so many that you overwhelm or frustrate your audience.

By the time you have carefully considered your artifacts in light of the selection criteria, you should have a varied collection of strong, objective-oriented materials that portray your best work in a multitude of formats. When you feel confident that you have accomplished the selection process, it is time to turn your attention to organization.

Organizing Artifacts

Organization is an extremely important aspect of portfolio development. In a traditional portfolio, all that is necessary is to determine the order of your objectives and the order of the artifacts within each corresponding section of the notebook. In electronic portfolio development, organization is a little more complicated but not difficult. When you begin the selection process, work your way through your collection of artifacts and make two decisions: the first is whether or not you want to include the artifact in your portfolio based upon the selection process previously discussed; the second decision is which objective the artifact supports.

Keeping your artifacts organized as you go is a tremendous time saver, and you should start organizing as soon as you begin collecting artifacts. Organize them in a logical way that makes sense to you. It is likely that you will need three collection methods: one for electronic artifacts, one for paper artifacts, and a third for materials, such as handicrafts, videos, and the like. It is helpful to create a folder on your computer's desktop to hold your electronic pieces. One or more manila folders or files are sufficient for your paper documents, and a cardboard box or plastic crate will work well for your remaining artifacts.

When the collection process is complete, refine your organization based upon the objectives of your portfolio. Within the Working Portfolio on your desktop, create a new folder for each of your portfolio's objectives (Figure 4.2).

Name them whatever is appropriate, as long as you know which is which. Similarly, create additional manila files or folders for each of your objectives, and divide your other artifacts in the same way. Finally, create one more folder, file, and box labeled "Discards."

Figure 4.2 Organization process for the working portfolio.

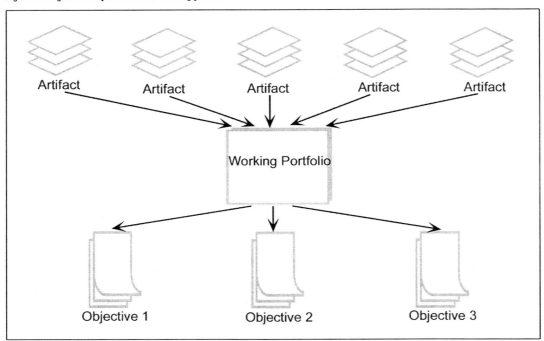

You will need to create three sets of folders similar to these: one set on the desktop of your computer for electronic artifacts, one set of manila folders for paper artifacts, and one set of boxes or crates for three dimensional artifacts. As you collect artifacts, put them in the working portfolio. As you select your artifacts, organize them by objective.

If you decide to omit an artifact, place it in the proper receptacle labeled "Discards." You are not actually discarding these pieces, but you want to keep them separate from the artifacts in the working folder until the selection process is complete. If you later change your mind and decide to include an artifact, it will be easy to find. Decide which of your objectives it supports and place it in the appropriate folder, file, or crate.

Invariably, you will consider artifacts that support more than one objective. Organize them according to the objective to which they are most closely aligned, noting the other objectives they document. Repeat this process as many times as it takes to make it through your collection until you are satisfied with your selection and how you have organized it. When you are done with the selection process, you will have folders, files, and crates for each of your objectives holding the artifacts that will ultimately be included in your portfolio.

This finalized collection is your ultimate response to the question, "What did I do?" You will answer the question again, addressing each artifact specifically as you begin writing your reflections.

Summary

The content of your portfolio is first determined by answering the question, "What did I do that pertains to one or more of my portfolio objectives?" The process of answering this question is the process of building the working portfolio. This collection consists of all the artifacts that support one or more of the portfolio's objectives. All types of materials, from awards to journal entries, may qualify for the working portfolio. It consists of pieces in electronic format, paper format, and other objects, such as videos, trophies, and handicrafts. These artifacts should be organized in electronic folders, manila files, and boxes that are labeled as working portfolios.

When the collection process is complete, it is time to answer the question, "What did I do best?" This question initiates the selection process. Now, is the time to evaluate each artifact in light of portfolio objectives, professional standards, and evidence of best practice. It is important to consider if the artifact relates to more than one objective, the type of artifact it is, and its format. The pieces that are selected in this process are placed in folders, files, and boxes according to the objective they document. When the selection process is complete, they are saved in the appropriate folders. With the collection and selection processes complete, the next step is to reflect on each artifact.

Chapter Five
Portfolio Development: What did I Learn?

In order for a portfolio to function as a vehicle for professional growth, the author must spend substantial time and energy answering the question, "What did I learn?" This question leads educators to thoughtful and critical reflections about how they practice their profession and why they do what they do. However, the term "reflection," as it is used in education today, conveys a variety of meanings. A clear definition is necessary before the reflection process can begin.

What Is Reflection?

"Reflection" and related terms have been used in education for several years. Many writers credit John Dewey with first integrating the concept of reflection with the practice of teaching. Another major influence has been the work of Donald Schön (1983), who uses the term "reflective practitioner" to characterize educators and other professionals who engage in reflecting about their practice "in action." Other researchers, such as Jack Mezirow, Kurt Lewin, and David Kolb, further theorize that reflection is a necessary element of adult learning (Figure 5.1).

Figure 5.1. An adult learning theory model.

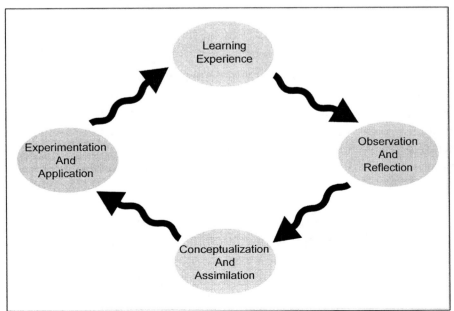

Learning from our experiences, according to many prominent adult learning theorists, involves observing and reflecting upon a specific experience, assimilating the observations and reflections into one's conceptual framework, and testing the resulting implications. This experiment results in a new learning experience, and the cycle begins anew. For more detailed information on adult learning theory, visit David Kolb's Web site http://www.learningfromexperience.com.

The literature is replete with articles defining reflection, describing the characteristics of reflection, and identifying strategies for reflection that will lead to professional learning and growth. Possibly as a result, reflection has become popularized, often to the point that it means nothing more than identifying what is or is not effective in the classroom. To the contrary, reflection and reflective practice are much more complex than the popular notion. Reflection that leads to authentic self-assessment and professional growth displays several defining characteristics.

- *Reflection links practice to knowledge.* Reflection is not just thinking for a long time or thinking a lot about a particular practice or activity. Reflection examines practice in relation to knowledge. Sources of knowledge should be many and varied: Personal perceptions are valuable, but input from others, such as colleagues and administrators, can provide insight as well. Our students can also provide a wealth of information, not just from test and homework grades, but from their own perceptions of what they learned from a particular activity. Reflection gives us the opportunity to relate our practice to theory, research, and standards of best practice, all excellent sources of information. The more knowledge we have at our disposal, the richer and more insightful our reflections will be.
- *Reflection examines beliefs and assumptions.* In order to reflect deeply and thoroughly, it is not enough to reflect upon our actions. We must move beyond what works and what does not in our practice and reflect upon *why* we practice as we do. Such assessment involves examining beliefs, assumptions, and attitudes that influence our professional mindset. Such thinking does not occur easily or quickly; it takes time, honest introspection, and self-knowledge to recognize the personal influences we bring to our work. Researchers point to a variety of strategies to help educators identify the beliefs and assumptions that underpin our practice. Activities such as, keeping a professional journal, writing an autobiography of our experiences with education, identifying personal teaching metaphors, reading professionally, and conducting ongoing conversations with other educators can help us know our professional selves better, which leads to more productive reflection.
- *Reflection is individual and contextual.* Although it is necessary to expand our knowledge of our practice by getting external perspectives and by professional reading, reflection remains an intensely personal activity. As important as research, theory, and best practice are, it is equally important to articulate our own thoughts and opinions about our practice. Such thinking should lead us to the core of our professional lives—the purpose of our practice. As we do this, we must extend our thinking to consider the contexts of our classrooms and our schools. Such reflection considers both internal and external influences on our thinking and practice.
- *Reflection is a process.* It is the process of getting to know ourselves professionally and then finding opportunities to grow. Reflection, to be truly helpful, should not be a once-a-year activity we complete as part of our evaluation. Reflection needs to be an integral part of our professional routine— one we regularly make adequate time for. Reflection is a difficult process on a

practical level because educators rarely are given time for reflection as part of their work day. Making time for meaningful reflection on a regular basis means exercising the discipline to give it priority when other responsibilities clamor for attention. Beyond that, reflection can be unsettling. It might mean recognizing aspects of our practice that are weak, or it could entail facing assumptions or beliefs we were not aware we held. Reflection often means moving beyond what is comfortable and stepping into new territory as we strive to master new competencies.

- *Reflection leads to professional growth.* The first purpose of reflection is to know ourselves better as educators. The second is to use that knowledge to embark on a career-long journey of professional growth. As we reflect, we are studying ourselves, not just to know ourselves, but to improve ourselves. Self-knowledge encourages professional growth. Growth encourages further reflection, which leads to more self-knowledge and more professional growth. In this way, reflection initiates a powerful cycle of knowledge and improvement that generates tremendous satisfaction and professional confidence.

Reflection can be described, then, as *the ongoing process of thoughtfully considering our practice in the context of our personal and professional knowledge, assumptions, and beliefs, with the aim of achieving insights that lead to professional growth* (Figure 5.2).

Figure 5.2. The reflective process.

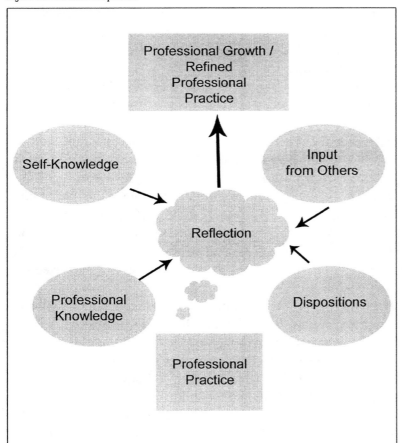

Reflection stems from our professional practice and is influenced by our professional self-knowledge, our knowledge of theory and best practice, our thoughts, attitudes, and beliefs, and the perspectives of colleagues, administrators, and students. Reflection then results in professional growth and improved practice.

Reflection and Professional Self-knowledge

Embedded in the definition of reflection is self-knowledge. It is important to know, not only our strengths and weaknesses in the classroom, but the motivations, assumptions, beliefs, and attitudes that influence our professional practice. These underlying influences can be discovered and identified by answering elemental questions such as: why am I an educator, what do I enjoy about my work, what do I dislike about my work, what are my professional strengths and weaknesses, what would I most like to change about my work, what is my role in the classroom, and how do I see my students and colleagues? These and related questions should be addressed before reflection on portfolio artifacts begins. This kind of self-reflection can be implemented using a variety of strategies:

- *Journal writing*. Keeping a professional journal can be one of the most insightful methods of self discovery. Whether we write daily or weekly, by class, subject, or unit, we can discover much about ourselves if we address issues such as what we did, why we did it, why we used the methodology we did, what worked and what did not, unexpected outcomes, and how we might improve next time. Thoughts, feelings, frustrations, anxieties, and successes are important components of journal writing as we explore feelings and attitudes. If this particular activity appeals to you, there are several good guides on the market including Larsen and Miller's (2003) *Day by Day: Professional Journaling for Library Media Specialists*.
- *Educational autobiography*. This activity is often used in teacher preparation classes to help students understand their motivations for becoming educators. It is helpful to reflect upon such educational experiences as what teachers influenced us as students, other influences such as friends and family, when we first considered education as a profession, when we "knew" we wanted to teach, our practice teaching, our first year experiences, and how we see our growth as educators.
- *Educational metaphor*. An effective tool to discover assumptions and attitudes is to identify our educational metaphor. Fill in the blanks: "In my classroom, I see myself as a(n) _____ ," or "I see my classroom as a(n) _____ ." How did you complete these sentences? Do you see your classroom as a science lab? What does that metaphor reveal about your practice? Do you see yourself as a gardener who nourishes her little flowers to grow and blossom, or maybe you are the curator of information in your media center. Whatever your answers, think through all of the implications and how they play out in your classroom. You might be surprised by what you discover about yourself.
- *Personal philosophy*. Articulating our personal philosophy of education is an excellent way to discover the convictions and values that underlie our professional practice. When we consider the beliefs we hold about children, education and what we value in our professional activities, we must carefully consider why we hold the convictions that we do. Doing so helps articulate a philosophy that will be personal, insightful, and meaningful.
- *Professional conversations*. All of the strategies suggested so far have been solitary activities. If they were the only self-awareness approaches taken, we

would benefit from only one person's point of view: our own. In order to consider other perspectives, we need to engage our colleagues in professional conversations. We might choose a trusted friend or mentor, an administrator, others in our content area, or a "mixed bag" of colleagues we know and respect professionally. Topics might be specific, such as, "I know you've used mixed grouping in Algebra I. I'd like to talk about how it might work for me in Basic Biology." The topic might be broad: "How can we help our growing ESL student population?" Sharing conversations such as these can help us recognize underlying beliefs, attitudes, and assumptions in ourselves and others.

• *Professional observations.* How often do you ask a colleague or administrator to observe your classroom in order to help you solve a problem, strengthen an instructional technique, or demonstrate a new methodology? Most educators would probably answer "Seldom" or "Never." Even if we were so inclined, most school-day schedules are not structured to foster collegiality. If we did, we could avail ourselves of a wealth of information; we could benefit not only from what our colleague observed, but from their professional insights. Conversely, observing the pedagogy of a respected colleague reveals much about attitudes, assumptions, and techniques we can then reflect upon in terms of our own practice. Functioning both as the observer and the observed can help us considerably as we seek to know ourselves.

Why Should I Reflect?

Regardless of the purpose for which a portfolio is developed, its key components are the reflections. If we know our professional selves well, then reflecting on individual artifacts can reveal our professional insights as no other practice can. This reason alone makes reflection a valuable endeavor. In addition, there are other significant reasons why reflection is a worthwhile activity.

Reflection reveals the context and importance of the artifacts we have selected to include in our portfolio. Without reflections, the portfolio would be little more than an organized collection of artifacts. Reflection contextualizes artifacts by describing how and when they were used, why we chose to include these particular artifacts, what they reveal about our practice, and what we have learned from them. No traditional résumé or evaluation instrument could relay such powerful personal information about our practice.

Because the artifacts that are included in our portfolios are self-selected, each portfolio is unique. Whereas many evaluation instruments and other forms of documentation are standardized, portfolios allow us to be pro-active in regard to documenting our accomplishments by selecting our own evidence. Because artifacts are unique, our reflections upon those artifacts are unique. The process of selecting one artifact over another begins the critical thinking necessary to examine and assess our practice. Reflecting takes the process even further, engaging us in deep, meaningful consideration of what we do, how we do it, and why. Such thinking gives us a voice to speak sincerely and convincingly through the artifacts and reflections in our portfolio. This aspect of the portfolio makes it truly our own.

When we take the opportunity to reflect on our practice, it is likely to improve. As a key element in adult learning, reflection helps us to consider alternatives or modifications to our practice, test them, and arrive at new or modified practices which we incorporate into our pedagogy. As we implement new methodology, we reflect upon it, and the cycle begins again. Over the course of a semester, a year, or a career, the cycle can spiral to ever higher levels of expertise.

Reflection is also an important element of professional portfolios because it is recognized as a professional behavior in national standards. INTASC, for example, links reflection and professional growth in its Standard #9. Likewise, candidates for national board certification must submit a portfolio, complete with artifacts and reflections that document the candidate's effectiveness in a wide range of knowledge, skills, and behaviors.

"(INTASC) Standard #9: The teacher is a reflective practitioner who continually evaluates the effects of his/her choices and actions on others (students, parents, and other professionals in the learning community) and who actively seeks out opportunities to grow professionally" (Campbell, Melenyzer, Nettles, & Wyman, 2000, p. 6).

Reflection is an important element of portfolio development for several significant reasons. It affords us the opportunity to effectively communicate our thoughts and feelings about our profession in a way no other instrument does and makes our portfolio intensely personal and unique. We grow professionally as we thoughtfully consider the several aspects of our pedagogy. As reflection becomes integrated into various national professional standards, it makes sense to adopt the practice as our own. Reflection should become a habitual element of our practice. Just as self-knowledge can lead to better reflection, reflection can lead to improved practice.

Reflection and Professional Development

Improving practice is the purpose of professional development. There are many theoretical models for professional development, but practically speaking, teachers generally recognize professional development as one of two types: either that imposed from without or that motivated from within. We have all been victims of the former—interminable professional development programs complete with a consultant or guest speaker who regales us with the newest methodology. This one-size-fits-all approach is seldom as effective as administrators hope.

An intrinsic desire for professional growth can produce substantial results. Perhaps you are a new teacher who is eager to grow. Possibly, you are a veteran educator who feels "stuck in a rut" and wants to try something new to make your career fresh and interesting again. Maybe, the idea of continuous professional growth sounds appealing to you, or you see it as part of your professional responsibilities. Whatever your reasons, professional development that is motivated from within can be instructive and rewarding, especially if it is developed within a reflective framework. The professional development portfolio provides that framework for reflection, and ultimately, for professional growth; however, every type of portfolio, regardless of its purpose, fosters professional growth because it includes reflection in the development process.

Reflection and the Professional Development Portfolio

The professional portfolio, and especially the professional development portfolio, can be a powerful tool for growth. It is this characteristic that primarily distinguishes the professional development portfolio from any other type of portfolio. Although it may be closely associated with an evaluation portfolio, the two are ultimately different. An evaluation portfolio is used by building, district, or program administrators as an instrument to judge skills and behaviors. The purpose of the professional development portfolio is personal professional assessment. It helps to determine the importance and value of our practice by focusing our reflections on specific artifacts that represent what it is we do. Reflection, in the context of the professional development portfolio, becomes a catalyst toward increasing our knowledge and skills.

"The quality of the learning that results from the portfolio development process will be in direct proportion to the quality of the self-reflection on the work" (Barrett, 2000c).

Reflecting for the Professional Portfolio

Understanding the concept of reflection and using it to discover professional self-knowledge prepares us for the reflections that are an integral part of the professional portfolio. How, then, do we reflect on the specific artifacts that we have selected for our portfolio? Keep in mind that reflections should answer the question, "What did I learn?" A three-part strategy can help you answer this question completely.

- *Reflect upon the artifact within its context.* The first section of the reflective statement should be a description of the artifact within its educational context. Describe what it is, the students you used it with, the unit of study, and how you used the artifact. This brief description should make the context clear to your readers.
- *Relate the artifact to standards, goals, or other criteria.* The second section of your reflection should convey why the artifact is important. Link it to standards, professional development goals, job requirements, or other criteria that your portfolio is designed to meet.
- *Reflect upon how the artifact impacted student learning.* Whether the artifact is a newsletter for parents or an article you published, link it to the effect it had on your students' learning and reflect upon its impact. If the first section of the reflection answers the question, "What?" then this section should address the question, "So what?"

These three sections of your reflection do not have to be lengthy, but they do need to show careful consideration of the artifact (Appendix C). Taken together, they should clearly and completely answer the question, "What did I learn?"

Summary

Reflection is the heart of a professional portfolio, unclear reflections purpose or portfolio, because it shows insight and leads to future growth. However, reflection is not necessarily an easy process. It must link what we do in the classroom with professional knowledge of theory and best practice. Reflection challenges us to examine our beliefs and assumptions that influence practice. Each person's reflections are unique because the process is individual and must occur within each of our individual contexts. If done carefully and thoughtfully, reflection on artifacts in the professional portfolio leads us to consider specific aspects of our pedagogy to determine the answer to the question, "What did I learn?"

Chapter Six
Portfolio Development: What Will I Do Next?

By now you have answered the questions "What did I do?" and "What did I learn?" In answering those questions, you have thoughtfully considered each particular piece within the context of your practice. You have thought about what you do in your position as an educator, how well you do what you do, and why.

Answering these questions has helped you develop a rich and textured self-portrait. You know your particular strengths and have identified weaknesses. Your self-assessment has provided a perspective of your professional practice, your professional beliefs and philosophy, and of your professional growth. Now it is important to use that self-knowledge to plan ahead. It is time to answer the question, "What will I do next?" (Figure 6.1).

Figure 6.1. Excerpts from sample artifact and accompanying reflection.

Artifact – Class Handout	Reflection
Interview Techniques	(What did I do?) This artifact is a handout of interview techniques that I developed for English III Communications in the Workplace students. This lesson was . . .
1 An interview is not a conversation between you and the narrator. You want the narrator to tell his story. Simply make a few brief remarks to break the ice and then ask questions that will guide him along.	
	(What did I learn?) The lesson was designed for students to practice speaking, writing, and listening skills as part of a unit on the Vietnam Conflict. After students observed a mock interview, they practiced formulating questions and recording answers. Students had difficulty developing good interview questions and were often recorded inaccurate information. I learned that students need more opportunities to practice their . . .
2 Be well prepared. Have your questions written out before you begin. However, don't feel that you have to ask all of them, especially if your narrator gives you relevant information that you weren't expecting.	
3 Ask questions that require more of an answer than "yes" or "no." Start with "why," "how," "where," "what kind of. . .," etc.	(What will I do next?) The sheet of interview tips was helpful; several students referred to it as they formulated their questions. However, I think that some students would do better if the tips were rewritten to be a little less wordy. I would reorder the tips since I now know that their biggest problem is avoiding "yes" or "no" questions. I will definitely use this handout again in this lesson because it did help them with reading, writing, and listening skills and engaged them in critical thinking, but I will try to give students more practice before their meeting with the veterans. Next time . . .
4 Ask one question at a time. If you ask a series of questions all at once, the narrator will probably only answer the first or the last question.	
5 Keep your question brief.	
6 Start with questions that are not controversial. Save the delicate questions for later in the interview when the narrator feels more comfortable.	

The question itself implies change is ahead. By considering your answers to this question, you are indicating that you are willing to consider change in your pedagogy. You are translating the insights gained from reflecting about your practice into actions. You are, in effect, laying the foundation for your own personal professional growth.

"Educators need to stop, reflect, self-assess, and redirect as needed in their pursuit of focus goals and professional growth" (Burke, 1997, p. 82.)

This type of professional development is powerfully effective because it is closely tied to the constructivist theory of learning. As constructivist learners, we use our current knowledge, information, and experiences as foundations for the formulation of new ideas, understanding, and meaning as we gain new information. Because we are constructing new knowledge within individual contexts, we can surpass the information at hand and answer the question, "What will I do next?"

Projecting Reflection

There are essentially two ways to answer this question: As you reflected on each of the individual artifacts contained in your portfolio, you first sought to answer the question, "What did I learn?" In order to answer this question completely, you described the artifact, the context in which it was used, and its purpose. Then you considered the artifact critically as you came to a conclusion about its degree of success. For example, you may have learned that the students really enjoyed the PowerPoint assignment associated with the unit on short stories, but they seemed to have missed the point of the assignment, and you did not get the results you were hoping for.

Now, to answer the question, "What will I do next?" you must consider what you know and decide how your practice should change. To fully answer that question, you need to dig deeper by examining some essential questions.

- *Did this activity meet the goals and objectives it was designed to achieve?* In reflecting upon your artifact, you may discover that, although the PowerPoint activity was creative and fun, it did not achieve your instructional objectives as you thought it would. If the activity the artifact represents was not closely associated with goals and objectives, you need to rethink the activity and modify your teaching strategy accordingly.
- *Did this activity meet the learning needs of all my students?* Children come to us with a variety of intelligences, skills, interests, strengths, and needs. It is a daily challenge to engage each child in the learning activities we use in our classrooms. To say it is difficult to stimulate and challenge each student to the best of her abilities is a gross understatement. We know, nonetheless, we must find ways to help each child flourish intellectually. Perhaps, then, you should reconsider that PowerPoint requirement. Possibly, it is not a good choice for every child in the

class. Maybe some would have liked to compose a song or an original dance, paint a picture, or tell their own story.

- *If I teach this lesson again, what will I change to make it more effective?* The artifacts included in your portfolio should be examples of your best work. They represent lessons that have gone well and activities that were stimulating and instructive. That does not mean, however, they cannot be better. Whether you have been in the classroom one year or twenty, you can always find ways to improve your pedagogy. Remember, when you select artifacts for your portfolio, you are selecting examples of best practice, not perfect practice. Your portfolio should show evidence of growth, not perfection. Identifying how you can improve your practice is evidence of your professional growth. You may have already decided to realign that PowerPoint assignment more closely with your goals and objectives. Maybe, you will give students a list of possible outcomes to choose from. Maybe, it is a terrific activity just the way it is, but you decide to develop it a step further by posting the students' PowerPoints on the school Web site.

- *Should I keep this particular activity/lesson/unit as part of my professional repertoire?* Over the course of our professional careers, we all consider and experiment with different instructional strategies, classroom management techniques, and curriculum materials. Some we reject out of hand, others we try and then discard, and still others we embrace and make them our own. As we seek an answer to this question, we consider whether the activity meets our instructional goals and objectives and if it engages our students in meaningful learning. However, we must consider if it suits our own individual teaching style. Although the activity may be perfectly fine for the teacher next door, if it does not "fit," then we should look for an alternative. When considering that PowerPoint activity, consider whether you enjoy teaching it. If not, why not? Is a lack of computer expertise the problem, or does it not fit with your pedagogical style? If computer skills are the problem, you may have identified a potential area for professional development. If it doesn't fit what you want to do with the lesson, then pass it on to a colleague who might enjoy it.

- *What have I learned from this lesson that will influence my pedagogy?* No matter what activity you are considering, know that it holds a lesson to be learned. The lesson you learn can be applied to the particular activity at hand, but it holds meaning for your pedagogy as well. The idea is to look at each artifact, consider each lesson or activity it represents, learn what you can apply to that lesson, and then consider how it applies to the rest of your teaching. What you are doing is refocusing on the big picture. Your PowerPoint activity may have spurred you to examine your integration of technology into your curriculum. By doing so, you may discover you use PowerPoint activities often but rarely incorporate any other computer skills. Possibly this is the only computer activity of the semester, and you know you should incorporate more technology into your instruction. Taking a broad view can reveal aspects of your practice you may have overlooked.

Once you have answered the question, "What will I do next?" for each entry in your portfolio, it is helpful to review your responses. If you have completed your reflections thoughtfully and critically, then it is likely you will discover some patterns in your teaching or general areas for improvement you will want to address. These areas are the foundation for formulating your goals and objectives for further professional growth.

Formulating Goals and Objectives for Future Professional Development

By refocusing our attention on the broader elements of goals and objectives, we can frame another answer to the question, "What will I do next?" Identifying patterns and trends in our pedagogy helps us formulate goals and objectives that will function as the organizational framework for future growth.

Planning ahead for future growth and development is important for several reasons. When you engage in critical reflection, you are looking at what you do in relation to what you know about teaching, your personal dispositions, and professional standards and goals. You are also considering current research, theory, best practice, and the thoughts and observations of peers, mentors, and administrators. As you examine these relationships, you will discover areas in which you want to change or improve your practice. You may find that you want to increase your expertise in your content area or update your knowledge about the practice of teaching. In order for you to strengthen these areas, you need to establish goals and objectives to guide your ongoing professional growth.

The goals you establish should stem directly from your portfolio reflections. They should refer to a specified period of time, such as a school year. If you prefer, you can work in larger or smaller increments of time, depending upon the goals you establish. Try to limit the number of goals you set. One may be sufficient, but more than three may be too overwhelming to accomplish in a reasonable period of time.

For each goal you set, develop a list of objectives. Each objective should be designed to help you achieve your goal, specific so you can know when you have completed them, appropriate to the time frame of your goals, and sufficient to help you meet your goal, but not so long as to undermine your efforts.

Let's say, for example, from the reflections in your portfolio, you have determined you would like to learn more about integrating technology within your content area. Your goal and objectives might read as follows:

Goal: Within the next year, I want to increase my knowledge and skill in integrating technology into the teaching of mathematics in my classroom.

Objectives:

- Attend the state *Technology in Education* workshop held in December.
- Read articles in on-line educational technology periodicals, such as *Syllabus* and *T.H.E. Journal* related to integrating technology in classroom instruction.
- Collaborate with the media specialist on developing a lesson using technology.

At first glance, these objectives may seem modest. However, it is better to set modest goals and objectives and achieve them than to set the bar too high and fail. Over the course of a professional lifetime, steady, planned professional growth will keep you current in your content area and keep your practice fresh, interesting, and challenging. Taking such an approach to professional growth will help you fulfill your responsibilities as a professional and will make your career more satisfying.

Thus, we have come full circle. We began by establishing a goal and objectives for our professional portfolio. We demonstrated our knowledge, skills, dispositions, and growth within those objectives by selecting and reflecting on specific artifacts that represented our practice. We then used those reflections to accomplish two purposes: first, to improve specific lessons and activities represented by the artifacts and our pedagogy in general, and second, to discern areas for continued professional development and growth. Based upon our findings, we formulated goals for future professional development and the objectives by which we will achieve those goals.

Summary

In this final phase of portfolio development we turn our attention from the past to the future. First, we look at the activities that our artifacts represent and determine what changes they prompt us to make in our lessons, activities, and practice in general. Then, as we recognize patterns or trends, we make decisions about goals and objectives for further growth and development. Formulating goals and objectives for professional development gives us a structure to guide our growth and development throughout our professional career.

Chapter Seven
Presentation and Production

Now it is time to focus on the "nuts and bolts" of portfolio development. The issues we have considered so far include the reasons for developing a portfolio, whether to create an electronic or traditional portfolio, what type of portfolio to develop, and its purpose, goal, and objectives. These issues should be considered by anyone interested in developing a portfolio; they are common to both traditional and electronic portfolios. If you have committed to an electronic portfolio, however, we need to make some production decisions particular to electronic portfolios alone.

One of the first decisions to consider is whether the portfolio will be a private document, accessible to only those persons you allow, or whether it will be public. If you decide to make your portfolio public, you will publish it to the Web; if you prefer to keep it private, you can make your Web site accessible by password only or publish it to a portable storage device, such as a CD-ROM. Next, you will conduct a self-analysis of your computer skills in order to gauge which technologies and software programs you will select for portfolio production. Finally, we will look at possible hardware and software development tools so that you can make your production decisions.

Presentation: Public or Private?

First, you will consider whether or not to make the portfolio publicly accessible by publishing it on the Web. In production terms, it is advisable to make this decision first because it will be a factor in your software selection. You should have in mind a clear destination for your portfolio, just as you have a clear purpose in mind. Being able to summon a mental picture of the final product can help you stay focused in a production sense, just as a clear purpose can help you stay focused in a developmental sense.

At first thought, the public or private question might seem easy to answer. If you are developing an evaluation portfolio, of course you want your portfolio to be private. Likewise, you would enjoy as large an audience as possible for your showcase portfolio, so a Web site would be desirable.

In deciding the public vs. private question, there are other issues to take into consideration besides whether or not to publish to the Web. You need to consider things like portfolio distribution, software and hardware issues, the computer expertise of your potential audience, your own expertise as a portfolio developer, and production challenges peculiar to Web pages. To make your portfolio public means to publish it to the Web. Keeping your portfolio private means you can publish it to the Web, with password restrictions, or publish it to a disk format of your choice, which you can distribute to your audience.

Public: Publishing to the Web

The easiest decision to begin with is whether or not to make your portfolio public. If, after careful deliberation, you decide you will, then you have made the decision to publish a Web site. Some readers may be horror-stricken: "Why would anyone want to do that?" There are several good reasons.

Consider the purpose of your portfolio. If the primary purpose of your portfolio involves input or reaction from others, as with a résumé or showcase portfolio, then it may be beneficial to have the portfolio accessible as a Web site. This way you can be fairly sure everyone interested can access your portfolio easily, wherever and whenever they want. Sometimes, you do not know who will be accessing your portfolio or even how many people will need to see it. If this is your situation, then a public portfolio may be the way to go. There will be no distribution problems to address, and the human resources director can examine your résumé on a Sunday morning at home in his PJs if he chooses. It makes sense to use a Web page to ensure accessibility by multiple users and flexibility of access by those who need to see it. If these are your main concerns, then seriously consider going public with your portfolio.

Before you make your final decision, however, there are other factors you should consider. First is the issue of hardware and software. To successfully produce an electronic portfolio, you need regular access to basic computer hardware and software. You also need to be sure your audience has computer access and is amenable to the idea of electronic portfolios. If you cannot affirm both conditions, then possibly your decision should not be whether or not to make your portfolio public, but whether or not to develop an electronic portfolio. If, after finishing this chapter, you decide you must take the traditional portfolio route, then you have made the additional decision to keep your portfolio contents private.

If you have the production tools, then take a look at your expertise in using them. Do not fall into the trap of thinking that if your skills and tools are basic, then you cannot create a portfolio that would be suitable for publication on the Web. Generally speaking, developing a public (Web) portfolio takes more sophisticated production tools and more expertise than a portfolio that will not be a Web site. Like any general statement, however, there are many exceptions. You may develop a technological wonder of a portfolio that you decide to keep private and distribute on disk. Possibly, you have only basic skills and equipment, but develop a perfectly serviceable Web portfolio. Your expertise is a factor, but not an overriding factor, in the public/private decision of portfolio development.

However, do not disregard this unbreakable tenet: **Do not try to learn more than one new thing at a time.** Learning how to develop a portfolio and at the same time how to operate complicated hardware or more sophisticated software at the same time, can be frustrating. If you feel you must incorporate new production tools into your portfolio development, then acquire them and learn how to use them well in advance of tackling your portfolio. You will save yourself headaches and frustration and avoid the serious risk of a missed deadline.

If you are considering publishing your portfolio on the Web, you will need to address the issue of where your Web site will reside. To be accessible on the Web, your portfolio must be saved on a computer that functions as a server to the Web. Depending upon the purpose of your portfolio, your district may allow you space on its server. If not, then you can check with your Internet Service Provider (ISP). Typically, they give their customers a nominal amount of server space to post personal Web sites. There are other avenues to free Web space available on the Internet, such as, <www.freewebspace.net>, or you can purchase the space you need for a nominal amount, usually on a monthly basis.

Private: Disk or Web?

If your portfolio will contain information you want to remain private or is sensitive in some way, you will want to restrict access to its contents. The decision to keep the portfolio confidential does not, however, mean you cannot publish it on the Web; it means if you do put it on the Web, you will want to use access restrictions, such as a password to ensure your portfolio is only viewable to those people to whom you have given access. Of course, all of the considerations mentioned previously that pertain to a public Web site are valid issues for a privately accessed site as well. However, a Web site is more easily accessible, and gives the user flexibility in terms of when and where to view your portfolio's content.

The other choice for keeping your portfolio private is to save it to a disk that can be copied and distributed to those who need it. Before you make this choice, there are some factors you need to take into account, such as your own expertise, access to production tools, and the needs of your audience. As with Web sites, you will want to consider the hardware and software selections that are available to both you and your prospective audience. Possibly, your portfolio is modest enough that it will fit onto a floppy disk, or you may want to burn it onto a CD or save it to a Zip disk.

You will make these decisions based upon the requirements of your portfolio and the hardware and software you and your audience have access to. If you decide to publish to disk, you must consider both hardware and software issues in relation to your audience. Not only must they have the hardware capabilities to open your disk, they must have the appropriate software installed to view the portfolio. You will need to know how to distribute copies of your portfolio to your prospective audience. You will need contact information, and you will need to make sure to have your portfolio copies distributed in a timely fashion.

Production: How Much Expertise Do I Need?

At this point, you are probably either feeling confident of your abilities to produce an electronic portfolio, or wondering if you have the technological savvy for the task. Believe it or not, you probably have much more knowledge than you realize and more than enough to create an electronic portfolio. You already create electronic documents if you create such things as tests, worksheets, and other documents in a word processing program, such as Microsoft Word and organize data in programs, such as Microsoft Excel. Perhaps you make multimedia presentations, such as PowerPoint slide shows. Electronic documents such as these can be collected and organized into your electronic portfolio. All you need are the technology and skills to accomplish the collection and organization processes.

The following table (Figure 7.1) is designed to help you identify your skill level so you can develop a portfolio that matches your expertise. Identifying the computing skills you already have and planning your portfolio development around them will reduce frustration later, and help you to be confident you are developing the best portfolio within your ability. You will be able to focus your efforts on your portfolio's contents rather than on its production, a strategy that should effectively help you achieve your purpose.

Figure 7.1. Levels of portfolio development expertise.

Level of Portfolio Development	If You Can . . .	Then You Will . . .
Basic	Use a word processing program, create folders, and save files	Use the appropriate software to collect artifacts and store them on a hard drive or a removable storage device, such as a floppy disk, CD-ROM, or a Zip disk. You will create and organize electronic folders to organize your artifacts.
Basic/Intermediate	Create a slide show or a simple hypertext document; create hyperlinks; import scanned images; import digital graphics	Use a word processor, hypermedia software, or slide show to organize and display the artifacts in your portfolio. Intermediate users will illustrate portfolios with imported or scanned graphics and create relationships among artifacts with hyperlinks.
Intermediate/Advanced	Record and import audio, record and import video, use Web page development software	Use Web page development software to organize and display your portfolio artifacts. Advanced users will supplement their portfolios with video or audio files.

Modified from Helen Barrett's Electronic Portfolio Development (2000b).

Production Hardware

Let's take a look at some of the hardware that you may want to use to develop your portfolio. The computer, of course, is a necessity, but it is the only one. It is possible to build a modest portfolio with no other hardware than your PC or MacIntosh. However, it must have sufficient hard drive space if you need to install additional software, and it must have enough RAM for the software to operate.

If you want to move beyond a basic portfolio, you will need other equipment (Figure 7.2). If you choose to distribute your portfolio on disk, you will need the appropriate hardware to create whatever type of disk you choose (for example, a Zip drive or a CD burner). If you are planning to include some paper artifacts that are not already in digital format—a certificate of achievement, for example—then a scanner will be a necessity. You may also decide you would like to use a digital camera to incorporate some photos into your portfolio. These are terrific options, but you do not have to invest in additional, expensive equipment in order to develop your portfolio. What you need may be available within your school or district.

Figure 7.2. Computer hardware for portfolio development.

Level of Portfolio Development	Hardware	Description
Basic	Computer	Your computer should have enough space on the hard drive and sufficient RAM to install and run any additional software you may need to create and save your portfolio.
Basic	A:\ Drive	Basic equipment on all but the newest computers. Useful for saving small amounts of data. Very basic portfolios may fit on a floppy disk.
Basic/Intermediate	Scanner	A scanner is required if you have paper documents or photographs that you want to save in electronic format for your portfolio.
Intermediate	Digital Camera	A digital camera is optional, but easy to operate. Usually, the camera's software must be installed on the computer you are using, although new memory card readers work with any camera. If you do not have access to a digital camera, you can scan regular photos.
Intermediate/Advanced	Digital Audio Recorder	With a microphone, you can record narrative directly into files such as PowerPoint presentations or add audio to other parts of your portfolio with hyperlinks.
Advanced	Digital Video Camera	You can add small video clips or streaming video to your portfolio. If you want to use a videotape, you will need conversion software and hardware.
All Levels	CD Burner	Most computers come with CD burners now. CDs can hold up to 700 MB of data. Rewriteable disks are more expensive, but allow you to make changes as you go.
All Levels	Zip Drive	Zip disks hold 100, 250, or 750 MB but can only be accessed by a Zip drive, which is not standard equipment on most computers.

Production Software

You will probably be incorporating more than one type of document into your portfolio. You may have several word documents, a spreadsheet or two, a slide presentation, and a variety of scanned artifacts. Regardless of how many types of documents or what format they are in, you will need one software program to provide the organizational structure for your portfolio. You will select one program to create the organizational pages of your portfolio, and everything you include—all of your artifacts, documentation, and reflections—will be organized within that program.

It is important to choose wisely. Think about the software that you use often and know well. Consider the purpose of your portfolio and the types of artifacts you plan to include. Then think about how to organize your portfolio. If you are unsure which software to select, create a few sample pages in various programs to see how they "fit." Usually, with some trial and error, you will be able to easily determine what organizational software will work best for you.

The following is a partial listing of some of the most popular software programs to consider for organizing your portfolio. Each program is rated as to the level of proficiency needed to use it effectively, its strengths and weaknesses for portfolio development, and some features you might want to look at if you are considering it for your portfolio. If you have another program you use regularly and fits the criteria for your portfolio, there is no reason not to use it instead.

"Many educators who want to develop electronic portfolios tend to design their own, using off-the-shelf software or generic strategies" (Barrett, 2000a).

Microsoft Word 2000, 2002

Proficiency Level. Whether or not you are a Microsoft fan, there is no escaping the fact that its software is virtually ubiquitous. Because it is so endemic, it has the advantage of being well known and widely used. If you are a Word user, then surely you will incorporate several Word documents into your portfolio. You can, in addition, use it as your organizing software if you are at the basic level of proficiency. If so, then rest assured you can use Microsoft Word to create a portfolio that looks professional and polished. Make sure you incorporate some of the software's special features to give your portfolio a finished look.

To use Microsoft Word as the organizational software for your portfolio, you should begin with a series of folders you create and save in My Documents or on your desktop. The folders should reflect the objectives of your portfolio, one folder for each objective. Each folder will hold the artifacts you select to verify knowledge, skills, dispositions, and growth for that objective. The artifacts you select do not have to be Word documents; it is possible to include other formats within the folders.

Strengths and Weaknesses. Because of its widespread popularity and use, you are probably already a proficient Word user. You can be fairly confident almost everyone in your audience has access to Word and knows how to use it. Pay attention to the version you are using; later versions can open earlier ones, but the opposite is not true. If you use a newer version than a member of your audience, he will not be able to access your portfolio. However, because it is easy to use, you will be able to create your portfolio with a minimum of time devoted to learning additional skills. Microsoft Word has some sophisticated features that can make your portfolio appear anything but basic.

The major weakness of using Microsoft Word, or any other word processing software, to organize your portfolio is that it is what it is—word processing software. It is not designed to function as a Web page program or multimedia software. Because of its versatility, Word has features that allow you to create multimedia or Web documents, but you will not find it as sophisticated or powerful as programs designed for those particular purposes. If you plan on a portfolio that is primarily text and some graphics, then a Word-based portfolio may work well for you.

Features. Figure 7.3 is an example of a portfolio main page created with Word. The background, colors, font sizes, and type style were automatically selected by choosing a Theme under the Format dropdown menu and by using the Style button. Word includes several themes to choose from; however, conventional wisdom suggests less is more, so you may want to stick with one of the more understated themes. If you would rather design your own portfolio, you can choose a Background, again under the Format dropdown menu. Borders are also available under Format, as are Bullets and Numbering, these are all great ways to help organize your material and give it a polished look.

Figure 7.3. Example of a main page created in Microsoft Word.

Professional Development Portfolio of Lester McCall

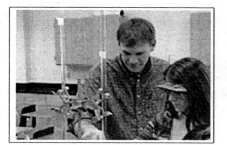

Personal Philosophy

Objective #1: Technology

Objective #2: Collaboration

Objective #3: Professional Growth

This portfolio was developed by customizing the background and the type color. Layout was designed using text boxes from the Drawing Toolbar and then eliminating the lines. Each heading is a hyperlink to a corresponding page. The photo was taken with a digital camera and inserted.

Another great place to explore in Word is the dropdown menu under Insert. Here you can add all types of items to basic Word documents. The photo in Figure 7.3 was added by inserting a "Picture from File." It is possible to add other files, symbols, a table of contents, and an index, just to name a few. If you are really ambitious, you can explore all of the possibilities under Objects; there you can insert video, audio, PowerPoint, and many other formats. Other useful tools in the Insert menu are Hyperlink and Cross-Reference. The Hyperlink tool allows you to link one document with another, and Cross-Reference lets you link to another section of the same document. You will find that these tools are extremely helpful in allowing you to create relationships among your artifacts and reflections. The headings in Figure 7.3 are hyperlinks to Word documents that, in turn, link to artifacts and reflections.

Inserting tables, with or without visible borders, is an easy way to organize and place text. You can make the table invisible by removing the lines, or you can highlight it by changing the background color. Other formatting options are available from the Format drop-down. A text box, found on the Draw tool bar, is another great positioning tool that allows you to place text or graphics anywhere you want.

If you are planning on publishing your portfolio to the Web, it is better to use Web development software, but Word allows you to save documents for the Web, and you should do so if that is where they are going to go. There are many other Word features you will find helpful in creating a polished professional portfolio. Generally, features are easy to use; remember, right clicking often gives you access to the command you need, and an extensive Help menu is readily available.

Microsoft PowerPoint™ 2000, 2002

Proficiency Level. PowerPoint is another "oldie but goodie" that can be used to organize your portfolio. Many computer users with intermediate skills are already adept at creating PowerPoint presentations. If this is you, then be assured you have the know-how to create a portfolio organized with this software. As with Microsoft Word, you will find PowerPoint encompasses a broad range of features, making it sufficiently flexible to produce a stylish final portfolio (Figure 7.4).

Figure 7.4. Example of a main page developed in Microsoft PowerPoint.

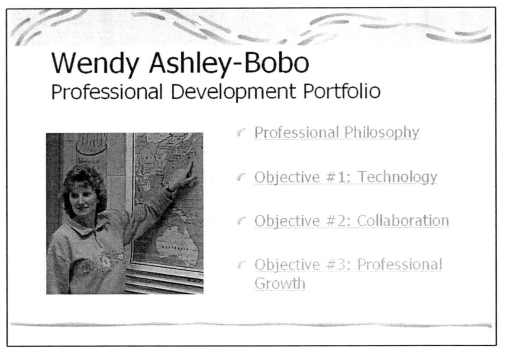

A theme was chosen to develop this portfolio in Microsoft PowerPoint. Hyperlinks were added to take the viewer to subsequent pages. Saving as a presentation eliminates the need for the viewer to open and then select Slide Show; the presentation will open in Slide Show format.

Strengths and Weaknesses. PowerPoint enjoys the benefit of universal use, so it, too, is probably already familiar to you and your audience. Even if you have had very little experience with it, you will find that it is easy to use and learn. You can quickly advance to sophisticated presentations that can be saved in several different formats, including a presentation that opens as a slide show (PPS file), and a Web page.

One difficulty you may encounter if you select PowerPoint for your organization software is that it is designed to be a visual program. You cannot and should not fit large amounts of text onto slides. In order for PowerPoint to work effectively with artifacts, documentation, and reflections that are primarily text-based, you will have to use hyperlinks to go to documents in other formats. If you do not anticipate much text on your organizational pages, then PowerPoint can work well.

Features. If you have access to PowerPoint 2002, one of the first features you will notice is the additional choices available in Slide Design and Slide Layout, giving you even more flexibility than earlier versions. Of course, it is always possible, and often preferable, to design your own slides, but whether you design an original or go with a design, keep in mind that you do not want the design to overpower the contents. With PowerPoint, users are often tempted by the vast array of animations and sound effects. You might want to use a few of these in an actual presentation, but they are best omitted from your portfolio.

Other features to investigate are the many choices available under the Insert menu. As with Word, it is possible to insert pictures, charts, tables, diagrams, text boxes, movies and sounds, and a vast array of other objects. It is also possible to insert slides from other presentations. Another nice feature, found under Slide Show, is the ability to add narration. You can even rehearse before you record. Of course, recording requires a microphone that plugs into your computer, and you will want to consider if your audience has speakers.

It is possible to insert hyperlinks in PowerPoint slides so you can relate the current slide to another slide in the presentation, a Web site, a new file, or an existing file. This feature gives you the flexibility of including all types of files in your portfolio while managing the overall organization with PowerPoint.

As with Microsoft Word, PowerPoint is packed with features that even experienced users may not have used. The Help feature and Index are extremely thorough and can assist you with virtually any problem you may have. It will be helpful to experiment a little before you begin your portfolio. Look at the program

Figure 7.5. Example of a main page created in Microsoft Publisher.

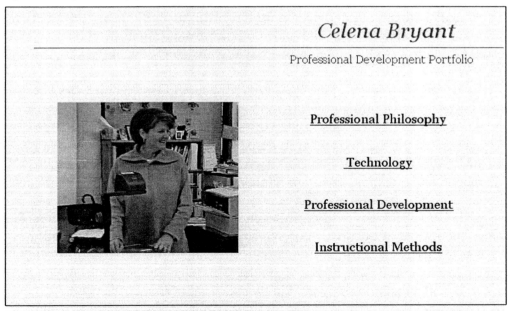

Publisher can be easy to work with and provides many tools, layout choices, and color schemes. This page was designed using a theme and then rearranging the page elements to fit the author's needs.

from a portfolio developer's perspective so you feel comfortable with it before you begin.

Microsoft Publisher™ 2000

Proficiency Level. You will find that Microsoft Publisher, like all Microsoft products, is packed with features. As the name implies, the purpose of this software is to create all kinds of publications. Using Publisher, you can design anything from brochures to greeting cards or anything in between. It also contains the features necessary to create Web pages (Figure 7.5). Microsoft Publisher is user-friendly with an extensive index, help menu, and a tutorial that walks the user through several of the software's features. Because Publisher includes a design Wizard for each of its publications, it might appear to be software that appeals to beginners only. However, more advanced users will find it offers sufficient flexibility to work for more sophisticated design requirements.

Strengths and Weaknesses. The biggest strength of Microsoft Publisher is its flexibility. If you are a novice, you can use the Web Wizard to design your site and all you need to do is work through the Wizard and then "fill in the blanks" with your content. However, if you choose to start with a blank Web page, you have a world of options to create your own design. Backgrounds, headers, navigation elements, color schemes, and much more are available for you to custom design your own pages. Every page element is contained in a frame and you design your pages by moving and resizing the frames. If you make a mistake, a pop-up tells you what you have done wrong. If you are already familiar with other Microsoft products, then much of the tool bars will look familiar to you, such as WordArt, Clip Art, drawing tools, and the like. Other elements, such as a hot spot button, tools to create forms, and HTML code will be new to you, but they are easy to learn and use.

The biggest drawback of Microsoft Publisher is that it is probably best to use this software only if you plan to post your portfolio on the Web. If you are publishing to a disk, then your audience must have Microsoft Publisher installed on their computers to be able to open and view your portfolio. Usually, Publisher is not included in the Microsoft Office Suite, so its availability for viewing may be limited.

Also, if you choose to use the Web Wizard, you will find that it works best if you do not try to make significant modifications to the layout. Because Publisher uses frames for Web page elements instead of tables, sometimes it can be hard to organize your layout the way you want it, especially if you do not have a lot of experience with the software. However, it is possible to move and resize frames, design elements, and graphics, and even remove individual frames altogether if you choose.

Another drawback you will notice right away is, even if you choose to make a Web page, the format of the document that appears on your screen is decidedly vertical because Publisher's primary function is to design print publications. When you use it to design a Web page and click on the Web Page Preview button, you see your page as it will appear on the Web, but there is a lot of vertical scrolling involved. You can change the page setup, of course, but all measurements are in inches or points (not pixels), so it takes some experimenting to get it right. If you want to try for screen-sized pages, your best bet is to start with a blank page, size it, and then design it yourself.

You will also need to be careful with colors. Since Publisher is designed primarily to create publications for the print medium and RGB values are not given, you cannot be sure all of the beautiful colors offered are Web-safe. This topic is explained in more detail in Chapter 8.

Features. In spite of these drawbacks, Publisher can be an easy and fun program to use. A very nice feature is the tutorial. If you have never used Publisher before, go to the tutorial (under Help) first. It explains how Publisher works and how to use many of the features.

For example, in Publisher, it is possible to create a background that can appear behind all of your pages. If you have design elements you want to repeat from page to page—a header, sidebar, or graphic, for example—you can put them on a background page and then use that background as the basis for all of your pages. Page navigation at the bottom of the screen lets you know what page you are working on and if you are on a page or the background.

Layout guides are also a helpful tool available from the Arrange button on the tool bar. Layout guides appear as pink and blue lines on each of your pages so that you can consistently design your pages. You can use the Snap To features in conjunction with the layout guides to assure precise alignment of your page elements.

Another great feature of Microsoft Publisher is the wide variety of ready-made page elements available in the Design Gallery. By going to Design Gallery Object from the Insert button, you have access to mastheads, navigation bars, buttons, side bars, and pull quotes, which are all designed to be used on Web pages. There are also features such as calendars, picture captions, and logos you can adapt to suit your Web page needs. A cautionary note: It is easy to get carried away with all of the great features. You will need to temper your selections by being mindful of the principles of good layout and design. A full discussion is coming in the next chapter.

If you are a Publisher user, then you may already have some brochures, pamphlets, or newsletters you have created as Publisher documents. If so, it is possible to convert them to Web pages within the Publisher software. This feature can be a tremendous time saver and another alternative to scanning.

Microsoft FrontPage™ 2000, 2002

Proficiency Level. FrontPage is perhaps the most widely used Web site creation tool available today. It creates pages according to the WYSIWYG method (What You See is What You Get), which means that what you type on the screen is what your audience should see when viewing your portfolio. This feature makes it easy for anyone to open the program and start making a Web page without any previous knowledge of HTML or Web design. Advanced users of this program will benefit from the HTML View tab found at the bottom of every page. It allows you to view the raw code that makes the page go. Overall, this program is easy to use for those with intermediate expertise but powerful enough to handle the needs of more advanced designers.

Strengths and Weaknesses. FrontPage enjoys vast success partly because a large percentage of Web users use Microsoft's Web browser, Internet Explorer. Because Explorer and FrontPage are both developed by Microsoft, they are highly compatible, and anything you produce in FrontPage should look the way you intend it to when viewed on Internet Explorer. However, you cannot have the same degree of certainty about the relatively small number of viewers who use Netscape Navigator. Fortunately, differences are usually negligible and are an unavoidable characteristic of Web design.

Ease of use is a major strength of FrontPage. You can open the program, start typing, and instantly have a Web page. All you have to do is save it. Images are easy to manipulate as well. Place them on the page wherever you like, and FrontPage will save them as placed, eliminating the need to know HTML in order to customize your more complex pages.

FrontPage does have a few weaknesses, however. The first is affordability. FrontPage is considered an extra in the Office Suite and may not be provided with your copy of Office. If you do not have it, it will cost approximately $150. However, nearly all versions of Windows come with FrontPage Express, which has many of the same features as the full version of FrontPage. To find out if your version of Office includes FrontPage Express, look in Program Files on your hard drive or conduct a Search. If you do not have it, you can find it on the Internet as a free download.

The second weakness involves the WYSIWYG feature. Sometimes what you see is not always what you get. You can spend more than a few frustrating minutes saving, viewing, tweaking, and re-saving to get your page to look the same on a browser (even Explorer) as it does in FrontPage. However, once you get accustomed to the quirks, FrontPage gets easier to use.

Features. FrontPage has a wealth of features but the basics will get you well

Figure 7.6. Example of a main page created in Microsoft FrontPage.

FrontPage is user-friendly and versatile. Beginners and veterans alike can create polished Web pages with this software. This main page was created by using a theme; the theme supplied the background, banner, and navigation buttons. A table was used to place the picture. Make sure to construct your portfolio in Navigation View first so that theme elements can be properly applied.

on your way toward a very nice looking portfolio (Figure 7.6). FrontPage has a lot of tools to make this process easy. In FrontPage 2002, the menu on the right is a valuable tool to help you get started. Choose Page Templates to see a list of templates for making your organizational pages. The "One column body with contents on left" is a great starting point that gives you plenty of room for text, a space for an image or two, and links on the left hand side for navigation. Whatever layout you choose, you will use the same one for all of your organizational pages so that your site is consistent and easy for your audience to navigate.

FrontPage's extensive menus offer many other features to help you design a professional portfolio. From the Insert menu you can choose everything from images to forms to customize your page. You can select a Theme to apply to the entire portfolio from the Format drop-down. Themes are installed with FrontPage, but you can also choose from additional free themes on the Microsoft Web site. New to the latest version of FrontPage is the integrated spell-checker, which corrects as you go. The Table menu gives you options to draw or define a table, which serves as a great resource to organize and format your information. Many Web designers recommend using tables in FrontPage to format all of the elements on your page.

Once you have your portfolio ready to publish, you have two options. You can publish it to the Web, or you can save it on a CD-ROM or other portable storage device. If you are going to publish your portfolio on the Web and you have space on a server, you can choose "Publish Web" from the File menu, which allows you to publish your portfolio to the Internet instantly. If you intend to publish to a disk or other portable storage device, your audience will view your portfolio on their browser.

Overall, FrontPage is an excellent tool for creating and organizing your portfolio. You can create simple pages or expansive Web sites, complete with themes and images to enhance the viewer's experience.

Macromedia Dreamweaver™ MX

Proficiency Level. Dreamweaver, unlike FrontPage, is aimed at the more advanced user (Figure 7.7). Perhaps, if you are already familiar with FrontPage, Dreamweaver will be easier to learn, but its target audience is the advanced user who is familiar with HTML. If you are that person, then Dreamweaver may be the software you choose to develop your portfolio. It has excellent resources for Web page designers (located on the right side of the screen labeled "Answers"), which contain extensive tutorials and helpful tips for beginning and advanced users alike.

Strengths and Weaknesses. Since Dreamweaver targets more advanced users, creating a portfolio with it might be a daunting task for anyone else. The program has a WYSIWYG design layout, but it is not the default mode. The default mode is a 2/3 layout view and 1/3 code view, which is more useful for a professional Web developer. Portfolio developers will (most likely) want to use the full layout mode which is accessed via buttons at the top of the screen.

A weakness for Microsoft users is that Dreamweaver does not have the familiar look of a Microsoft Office Suite product. If you use nothing but Microsoft software, developing your portfolio will involve learning the idiosyncrasies of new software as well as getting used to new menus, buttons and options. For example,

Figure 7.7. Example of a main page created in Macromedia Dreamweaver.

Polly Brown-Bentley
Professional Development Portfolio

-Professional Philosophy

-Objective #1: Technology

-Objective #2: Collaboration

-Objective #3: Professional Growth

This main page was created in Macromedia Dreamweaver Web development software. It is the most sophisticated program considered here and is suitable for advanced users only.

Dreamweaver locates the text formatting options at the bottom of the screen instead of the top. Looking for various tools and commands can be time-consuming and stressful if you are new to the program. New users will need to allow for significant learning time to become proficient. Those of you who are more comfortable with the Office Suite menu layout will probably want to stay with FrontPage.

However, sophistication is also an advantage of Dreamweaver. Advanced Web page designers can easily take advantage of its multitude of options, from applying cascading style sheets (CSS) to inserting code such as Javascript, Hypertext Preprocessor (PHP), or Active Server Pages (ASP). Dreamweaver always keeps advanced options to the left side of the screen and basic options at the bottom, so you will not have to look very long to find what you need.

Features. Dreamweaver's many features include several menus from which you can insert commonly used items such as tables, forms and scripts. The Insert menu includes all the standard elements as well as many advanced options. For designing a new Web page, Dreamweaver provides several templates when you click File, then New. Choose Page Designs for all the templates you will ever want. If you decide to design your page yourself, you can save it as a template too.

Dreamweaver's overall design concept seems to be "provide everything possible." The program includes a multitude of options under the Text menu— everything from alignment to color, size, indention, and block quotes; everything you will need for text is under this menu. If you have a problem, you will find excellent tutorials and the complete O'Reilly HTML reference for advanced users.

Saving and publishing your Web page is easy in Dreamweaver. You can save as an HTML file, or you can publish your files much like you would in FrontPage. You can also use an external FTP program if you prefer.

Dreamweaver is an excellent program for Web design, but it may be too daunting for beginning or even intermediate users. Its excellent resources and built-in reference materials are great for advanced users or for those who may want to learn more about Web design.

Knowledge Adventure HyperStudio™ 4.5

Proficiency Level. HyperStudio is a multimedia program that creates everything from Web pages to executable files and runs on any Windows PC (Figure 7.8). Projects created in HyperStudio are defined as stacks, while cards are the pages within the project. This program is marketed for elementary classroom use and should be easy to learn and use for those with basic skills. However, HyperStudio has a daunting menu bar with choices that are sometimes confusing. If you are new to the program, expect to spend considerable time learning basic functions and even more time experimenting with the basic layout and design.

Figure 7.8. Example of a main page created in Knowledge Adventure HyperStudio.

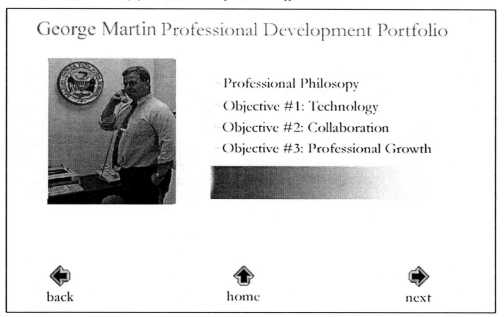

This is a HyperStudio card. All the portfolio organizational pages would constitute a stack. You can select a theme for your stack that gives it a distinctive look and allows you to insert objects you design like these navigational arrows.

Strengths and Weaknesses. A weakness of HyperStudio for portfolio development has to do with the way the program saves stacks. A HyperStudio stack can be saved in three ways: It can be saved as an STK file which can only be viewed in HyperStudio or with the Web plug-in available for download from the HyperStudio site. The plug-in works well for viewing STK files, but a disadvantage is that viewers have to know the exact Web address of your STK file, not just an easy-to-remember domain name. The second way to save is as an EXE file. If saved as an EXE, your portfolio will not be very easy to distribute because you cannot put an EXE file on a Web page, except for download. Most viewers will not download an unknown file, even from a trusted individual. E-mailing your file is not prudent, as most e-mail clients are configured by default not to accept EXE attachments.

Since distribution of your portfolio is crucial, that leaves publishing on the Web. "Export to Web page" is located under the Extras menu, and is somewhat hard to find. The resulting Web page is only viewable if you save the HTM file in the same directory as your stack file, meaning you have to upload both the HTM file and the STK file to the server. Fortunately, the program reminds you of this before you save. However, your audience must have HyperStudio or the plug-in installed to view your portfolio on the Web.

Another disadvantage to HyperStudio is how it handles layout and design. The menu system is non-intuitive and offers no tool tips (popup windows which explain the function of a menu choice). If you are not already familiar with the HyperStudio menu, it will take some time to locate and learn how to use the various functions. The user is left to experiment when a simple popup window would save considerable time. Also, once you choose a size for your cards, every card has to be the same size; there is no allowance for different screen resolutions.

Finally, there is a problem in the way HyperStudio handles files. If you insert a sound or video file into a HyperStudio presentation, the file is not added to the stack, but merely referenced from its original location on the hard drive. Therefore, any audio or video files you intend to publish to the Web will not load unless you save them in the same directory as the rest of your portfolio

Features. HyperStudio offers three options at the opening screen along with a Tip of the Day on the left side. The three options are: "Create a new stack," "Open an existing stack," or "Go to the home stack." If you are new to HyperStudio, the third option is best for you. Although the name is somewhat vague, the home stack contains clickable links that lead to tutorials and other helpful links. It is important to note that HyperStudio does not let you position the program window on the screen. Once you click one of these options, the window will move back to the center of the screen, making it extremely difficult to multitask while using the program.

HyperStudio comes bundled with several ready-made cards which are designed to give you an idea of what a good card looks like. They are not templates. To make a new card you will have to start from scratch. You may want to design your own card anyway since most of the pre-made cards are geared toward elementary classrooms. For professional portfolio development, you will want to find or make your own graphics.

HyperStudio has a nice selection of fonts, all located under the Format menu. If you do not like the normal fonts, the program comes with several custom ones like Royalbrush and Import, which are both stylish and professional looking. Most of the other fonts are geared towards younger users of the program.

The Objects menu has many useful features such as, the "Add a Button" option, which lets you design your own custom button for navigation links, "e-mail me" buttons, and more. There are no presets, though, so you will have to design your own from scratch. Other handy features include a built-in spell checker, Navigation Helper, and Title Card maker.

Once you have completed all of your cards, you save the complete presentation as a stack. Under the File menu you can choose Slideshow, which will take you on a tour of your cards. The slideshow can be configured however you like, including the interval between slides. Unfortunately, you cannot manually control this feature; your show has to proceed in set intervals, which makes it hard to configure for presentations.

Overall, HyperStudio's lack of presentation options and cumbersome menus do not make it a viable alternative for portfolio development. A more complex program is probably needed, but if your portfolio needs are simple and you are familiar with HyperStudio, you may be able to develop an adequate portfolio.

Other Software Programs

You will find that other software programs will be helpful in developing your electronic portfolio. If you rely exclusively on clipart and other built-in functions without adding your own pictures, audio, or even video, your portfolio will lack the distinct personality that says it belongs to you. What follows is a brief discussion of some of the most common programs and how you might use them to develop your portfolio.

Microsoft Excel™ 2000, 2002

Proficiency Level. Although you will not use Excel as your organizational software, its usefulness is worth including. Excel is the premier spreadsheet tool for Windows, offering not only the ability to calculate complex formulas but also the ability to transform numbers into meaningful representations in the form of graphs and bar charts. Excel has been around since the early days of Microsoft Office, so many users will already be familiar with its basic functions. If you can create a basic spreadsheet in Excel, then you can quickly learn the intermediate tasks necessary to create eye-catching graphs or charts. Most users of Office who are not familiar with Excel will still be familiar with the Windows layout and will benefit from the excellent help files and documentation provided with the program to guide them through more advanced tasks.

Strengths and Weaknesses. Excel is an excellent tool for adding visual interest and appeal to your data. Excel integrates easily into any other program in the Office Suite, so, importing a graph or pie chart is as simple as Copy/Paste. You probably will not be using Excel for many of your portfolio entries unless you have extensive mathematical content to present, so, its easy learning curve is great if you want to produce a graph or two and move on.

Features. Excel has a wealth of features that will make the creation of spreadsheets for your portfolio easy. One of the most important is the template. Select the File menu and choose "New." If you have Excel 2002, a menu on the right side details options. The most valuable options are listed under the "New from Template" heading. You can choose from general templates, ranging from expense reports to timesheets, but you will also want to select "Templates on Microsoft.com." From this Web site you can download hundreds of useful templates for your portfolio. Once you have decided on a template and entered your data, you can save it in almost any format you wish. Then, it is simply a matter of copy and paste to insert your file into your portfolio.

If you would rather not use the templates, Excel has several other options to explore. The Insert menu is an extremely useful resource and can often be a great starting point. Listed under the Insert menu is "Function," which offers a vast array of choices for performing calculations on your data. Some examples are "sum," "average," "mean," and "count." These functions provide a quick, error-free alternative to long manual calculations.

Also, under this menu you will find the Chart option which is an easy-to-use wizard for organizing your data. Options range from pie charts to line graphs, making it easy to find something that will perfectly fit your portfolio needs. Perhaps you would like to illustrate how much circulation has increased in your media center over the past few years; a bar graph might be the answer. Maybe, a pie chart can best illustrate the reading levels of your fourth-graders. Excel can help you illustrate the important data you want to include in your portfolio. Excel is a great complement to other Office programs and can also be used on its own for great-looking charts and graphs. For electronic portfolio development, Excel is a dynamic way to visually crunch your numbers for professional-looking results.

Adobe Acrobat™ 5.0

Proficiency Level. Adobe Acrobat software is another possible program to use in developing your portfolio. Acrobat has the advantage of being easy to use and easily recognizable. Most computer users have accessed documents created in Acrobat via Adobe's free download of Acrobat Reader. Acrobat files are saved as PDF files (portable document files) that make them portable. Creating them and accessing them can be as easy as a click of the mouse. For this reason, if you have access to and experience with Adobe Acrobat, you may want to consider using it in your portfolio.

Strengths and Weaknesses. Adobe Acrobat's strongest asset is that its PDF files can be accessed on Windows, Mac OS, and UNIX platforms. All it takes is Adobe Reader, which most computer users already have installed; if not, they can easily download it from Adobe's Web site.

Acrobat files are easily created by converting files from other formats. In Microsoft Word, for example, it is possible to convert a document to PDF format with a click of a button. Other files can be "printed" using the Adobe Distiller, which comes with the software package. Artifacts that are scanned can be directly imported to Acrobat from the scanner. Converted files and scanned items retain all their original properties including formatting, layout, and graphics. Thus, the PDF files look exactly like the originals, have the uniform look of PDF documents, and can be opened by anyone who has downloaded Adobe Reader.

The most apparent drawback to using Adobe Acrobat is that two separate software programs are required for creation and access. Also, the file size of PDF documents is rather large, although this should not be a factor if you are saving to a CD-ROM or other high capacity storage device. Acrobat is not a Microsoft product, so if all you use is Microsoft and you are just learning Adobe Acrobat, give yourself some time to get accustomed to a different look and features. Remember, that this program is not used to create new files but to convert existing files to PDF format. You will not use it to create your organizational pages unless you create them in another program and then convert them to PDF files. Also, be aware that you must purchase Adobe Acrobat; it is not part of the free download of Adobe Reader.

Features. The best feature of Adobe Acrobat is the ease with which you can create PDF documents. In Microsoft Word you can click the "Convert to Adobe PDF" button on the toolbar. In other applications, select Print and choose Adobe

Distiller to create your file as a PDF. If you have documents, photographs, or graphics to scan, simply open Adobe Acrobat and select Import from Scanner. Your paper artifact becomes a PDF file quickly and easily.

Conversely, it is also possible to convert PDF documents to word processing software by saving files in rich text format (RTF) that can be read by Microsoft Word or other software applications. Graphics can also be converted from PDF format if necessary.

Another great feature of Adobe Acrobat is you can provide a variety of ways to navigate among your documents. Each Acrobat document generates miniature versions (thumbnails) of its pages so the user can easily navigate to any page in the document. Additionally, it is possible to add hyperlinks to pages within the document or to other documents. You can also add a searchable index that covers multiple PDF documents. Security is another feature you might like. If you select Document Security from the File menu, you can then choose the security options that are right for you. That way, you can be assured your portfolio contents do not get altered.

Image Editing Software

Image editing software programs range from free to expensive, and simple to sophisticated. What you use will depend upon the type and extent of graphics editing you will need to do. Probably, most of your image editing work will be resizing images and correcting the color. If that describes your needs, then you might want to use Microsoft Photo Editor. Photo Editor performs basic functions like rotating, cropping, and color correction but lacks the tools necessary to finely tune images or add fancy special effects. If your images do not need much touching-up, this is an excellent program to use, and you probably already have it as part of the Office Suite. However, if your images need extensive editing, or if you want to add special effects, you will need a more sophisticated program.

Adobe Photoshop Elements is an excellent photo-retouching tool that can perform all the basic functions and offers more options than Microsoft Photo Editor. With Photoshop Elements you can correct color, blur images, and add borders for example. This software is reasonably priced and can be found at many Web sites at an educational discount. The companion program, Adobe Photoshop, is used by many professionals; it offers many more features but is also more expensive. Consider this option only if you are a graphic artist and need to both edit and create graphics. If not, a simple program like Microsoft Paint (included with Office) will probably fill your graphic design needs.

Audio and Video Software

You may also decide to add interest to your portfolio with audio or video files. Keep in mind not every computer has the same software for playback, so try to limit your audio/visual content and make it an optional part of your portfolio's contents. For WAV files that can be inserted into a presentation, the sound recorder in Windows can record and save the audio files you need. To compress these files, Windows Media Player includes a tool to convert them to the popular MP3 format. Media Player also comes standard with a utility to capture your digital video and save it as an AVI or MPG file. MPG is more stable, versatile, and compatible than

AVI, so you can be confident the file will be accessible to your audience.

Real Player is also an option for inserting audio or video into a portfolio. There is a free download of Real Player, but producing streaming content requires a purchase from Real Networks. Be aware if you use Real software, pop-ups will appear on the screen in addition to your content. The programs run slowly and are difficult to install without the accompanying spyware. In addition, your audience must have Real Player installed to view or listen to any files you have created with a Real product. You will be better served using Microsoft Media Player for your audio and video needs. If you are still interested in Real Player, however, and want to examine the software yourself, you can find it at <www.real.com>.

Summary

Before you consider what your hardware needs might be and which software you will use, take the time to carefully decide whether your portfolio will be published on the Web or to a disk. If you want your portfolio to remain private, you have the choice between a secure Web site or publication to a disk. If you want your portfolio to be available for public viewing, then Web publication is the right choice.

If you want to publish to the Web, then you should use Web page software if at all possible. Other software programs will work but not as well. If your portfolio will be private, consider a secure Web site. If you would rather publish to a disk, then you need to make sure the software you use is also a program your viewers have available. The notable exception to this rule is Adobe Acrobat, which uses the free download of Adobe Reader to open PDF files.

These are important decisions to make. Make sure you get it right by carefully considering your portfolio needs, your expertise, hardware and software availability, the features and limitations of the various software programs, and the needs and restraints of your audience. Once you have determined what software you will use to produce your portfolio's organizational pages and how your portfolio will be published, you are ready to consider how you will develop its layout and design.

Chapter Eight
Portfolio Design Basics

Once you have chosen the organizational software for your portfolio, you can begin the production process. You have already organized your artifacts and reflections according to your portfolio's goal and objectives. Now, you are ready to construct the organizational pages for your portfolio and transfer your artifacts and reflections into your portfolio. As you build your portfolio, you will find you have several design decisions to make along the way.

> "Anyone can learn the mechanics of making a Web page. And anyone can make an ugly Web page. Lots of people do. But the only reason so many people make bad Web pages is that they don't understand the very basic design principles" (Williams & Tollett, 2000, p. 105).

When considering the design elements of your portfolio, first look at its structure, or how the contents are organized. Once you have determined the structure, decide the basic layout of your organizational "pages." Your main page, the page for each objective or standard, and any other organizational pages should have a consistent layout in order to provide unity to your portfolio. As you make decisions about the layout, consider design elements such as alignment, proximity, repetition, and contrast. You will also need to make decisions concerning color, graphics, navigation, and type. The concepts involved are simple but will make a huge impact on your finished portfolio. They will result in either a well-structured, pleasing, and attractive portfolio or a hodge-podge of poorly designed documents your audience may quickly abandon in frustration.

Structure

As you defined your goal and objectives, you were laying the groundwork for your portfolio's organization. If you haven't done so already, you should commit your organizational structure to paper. Doing so will help you stay organized during the production process, and it will help ensure that your portfolio's structure is logical, inclusive, and easy to navigate. An easy way to experiment with structure and organization is to use a Post-it® note for each of your objectives and artifacts and affix them to a large sheet of paper. You can easily arrange and rearrange the Post-it® notes until you achieve the overall organization that is the most logical and displays your artifacts in the best light.

Usually, a hierarchical arrangement works best to organize objectives and artifacts. However, it is possible to use a linear structure that would be similar to a traditional portfolio. Whatever structure is selected, relationships between objectives and between objectives and artifacts should be characterized by hyperlinks. Hyperlinks make it possible to demonstrate complex relationships between objectives and multiple artifacts, between artifacts and multiple objectives, between objectives, and between artifacts. Navigation buttons should make it easy to return to each objective and to the main page from anywhere in the portfolio.

Layout

Another way you need to think about the organization of your portfolio is to think of the layout of the individual "pages" in your portfolio. You need to remember your portfolio will be displayed on a computer screen, not on paper. No matter what software you have selected to organize your portfolio, its contents will be displayed in a more horizontal format than it would be if it were on paper.

If you are using a program such as PowerPoint or HyperStudio, your slide or card is already sized to fit the screen. However, if you are designing a Web page, you will need to size your pages within the standard 640 x 480 pixels so the pages will be completely viewable on any size monitor and at any resolution. Your main page should fit entirely within this space so that no scrolling is necessary. It is acceptable for your audience to scroll down on subsequent pages, but under no circumstances should you make them scroll horizontally. If you have trouble experimenting with the layout on the computer screen, use the template in Appendix D as a guide.

Another point to remember if you are developing a portfolio to publish on the Web is you cannot be completely in control of what your audience will see on their computer screens. Users are able to set their own browser options, including turning off graphics, so you will need to keep your layout and design as simple as possible.

Alignment

Alignment is the act of lining up the elements on a page along a common invisible line. If you are familiar with Microsoft Word, you have, no doubt, used the "align left," "center," and "align right" buttons on the tool bar to achieve the vertical alignment you want. When you align left, for example, every line is flush at the left margin. Similarly, when you align on the center, every line is centered within the margins of the page.

Although it may be fine to mix alignments on paper, such as centering a title over a manuscript that is aligned left, it is not fine to mix alignments on your computer screen. To do so gives your content a disorganized, cluttered appearance and can make it hard to follow. In order to avoid this common mistake, pick one alignment and use it consistently throughout the organizational pages of your portfolio.

If you have a large amount of information or data on a page, it is probably better to select a flush left alignment rather than a centered alignment. Centering works well and looks attractive but usually only for small amounts of text. Aligning your text and graphics flush left makes it neater and easier for your audience to follow. You do not have to align everything on the same vertical line; your page can have more than one flush left, as when you use tabs or tables. However, all your material—text and graphics—should align left. Visual clutter starts to accumulate when you combine flush left with center alignment (Williams & Tollett, 2000).

Unfortunately, many Web page designers do not follow this basic concept. Surf the Web and look at some of your favorite pages; you will quickly find several examples of pages with mixed alignments. Look at the pages critically and you will see that the different alignments distract from the page's contents. Find a page that uses only one alignment and you will immediately notice the improvement in terms of readability, organization, and attractiveness.

Horizontal alignment, or alignment along a common horizontal line, is also important. If you have ever constructed a table with several headings, you have probably encountered the issue of horizontal alignment (Figure 8.1). You will find information looks neater and is easier to read if it is aligned along a common bottom line or baseline. Some software programs give you the baseline option for alignment; if the option is not available, you have to achieve the alignment manually. In either case, you will find it is a simple way to give your page a neater look.

Figure 8.1. Examples of incorrect and correct horizontal alignment.

Levels of Portfolio Development	If You Can . . .	Then You Will . . . .

There is no common baseline for the headings in these cells.

Levels of Portfolio Development	If You Can . . .	Then You Will . . . .

There is a common baseline for the headings in these cells.

Proximity

Proximity refers to the relationship among the various parts of your page. If items are grouped closely together, then they have close proximity, which makes them appear to have a relationship with each other. If there is substantial space between them, then it looks as if no relationship exists. The trick is to recognize which elements on a page should be in close proximity and which should not.

Some page elements come readily to mind. For example, a caption should always be in close proximity to its graphic. Similarly, a heading or title should be placed near the body of text to which it refers. By grouping related items close together and leaving space between elements that are not related, you are organizing your information and making it easier for your audience to read. This technique gives a purpose to the space you have on your page; the space is there to create a disassociation between elements, just as proximity creates a relationship. Using this technique in conjunction with proper alignment can give your page an organized and attractive look (Williams & Tollett, 2000).

Figure 8.2. Examples of poor and effective repetition.

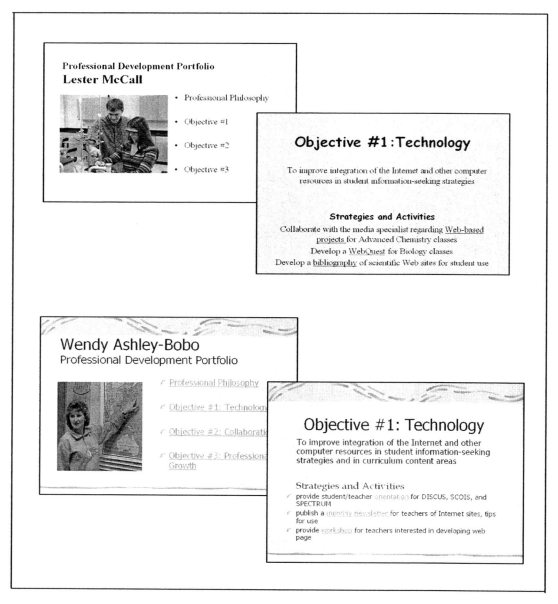

The first pair of slides has little in common although they are part of the same portfolio. The first slide has strong vertical alignment, a neutral background, and a consistent font. The second slide uses a background that interferes with the type, two fonts, and a centered layout. These slides do not appear to belong together because there is little repetition of design elements. In contrast, the background, alignment, colors, and type in the second set of slides are strongly repetitive, achieving a unified look.

Repetition

Repetition is the technique that brings unity to your portfolio. Your portfolio, no doubt, consists of a variety of artifacts in a variety of formats. You probably have text documents, graphics, documents in PDF format, and maybe a slide presentation or two. Such variety is expected, even desirable, in a professional portfolio, which is all the more reason why you need strong, repetitive elements on your organizational pages (Morris, 1999).

You can create repetition in your portfolio in a variety of ways. Alignment, layout, color, type style, graphics, backgrounds, and hyperlinks can be used, individually or in combination, to create a sense that all of the pages of your portfolio belong together. When the same elements repeat from one organizational page to the next, your audience recognizes the repeated elements, is already familiar with those elements, and will feel comfortable using the new page. Repetition helps your audience know what to expect instead of surprising them with new fonts, layout, background, or colors.

For example, the first set of pages in Figure 8.2 are part of the same portfolio and were created in Microsoft PowerPoint. However, they do not look as if they belong together because of the lack of common elements; there is little repetition from the main page to the next. However, the second set of pages look as if they belong together. There is unity between the two pages because the repetitive elements unify them.

Repetition can be easily achieved by selecting a theme in a Microsoft product, such as Word, PowerPoint, FrontPage, or Publisher. Themes have the advantage of consistently repeating design elements such as background, type style, size, and color to achieve a strong unity among pages. However, you need to be careful when selecting a theme so you do not choose one that is overpowering and distracts from your content.

You can also opt to use cascading style sheets (CSS) to design the organizational pages of your portfolio. Cascading style sheets are stored as separate files that, when applied to your pages, apply the design parameters you have established. When you choose to work with cascading style sheets, you have the advantage of being able to make changes to the style sheet that are then made on the pages you specify.

Contrast

Contrast can be created using several elements on your page. You may have contrasting type, color, font size, or graphics. Contrast is used as an organizational tool by creating a hierarchy of the elements on your page. After you establish a focal point for your page, whether it is a title or a graphic, the remaining elements are organized according to their importance. You can accomplish this by using a contrasting font style or size, a different color, or some other type of contrast (Williams & Tollett, 2000).

Generally speaking, if you want to provide a contrast between elements on your page, make the contrast striking. If you design elements to look almost the same, you defeat the purpose of the contrast and reduce the organizational effect. It is important to use contrast to clearly identify the focal point of the page and then use it to group remaining elements in descending order of importance.

Sometimes, however, you do not want much contrast on a page, especially if you have a large amount of continuous text you want your audience to read. Clearly, in this circumstance, contrast would be distracting. However, on the organizational pages of your portfolio, you will want to use contrast to organize the contents and help your audience navigate through your portfolio.

It is important to use contrast in conjunction with other design elements, such as proximity, alignment, and repetition, in order to achieve the effect you want. For example, you might establish your focal point and then, using other design elements, repeat colors or type styles in subsequent sections that are defined by alignment and proximity to organize the page.

Navigation

With a traditional portfolio, navigation is not much of an issue. Make a nice set of divider tabs for your notebook and you are done. With an electronic portfolio, however, navigation is much more complex. Without a clear, logical, user-friendly navigation design for your portfolio, your audience could become confused and frustrated. Your goal is to make navigating your portfolio so easy the navigation system itself is virtually unnoticeable.

Navigation throughout your portfolio is accomplished with a navigation system. It may be text or graphics—the choice is yours. Which one you choose is mostly a matter of aesthetics, but your navigation system must be consistent and clear. Navigation buttons or bars should be in the same place on every page and should look the same on every page. Your viewer should always be able to tell exactly where she is in your portfolio. These are the hallmarks of a good navigation system. Through good use of layout techniques, repetition, proximity, and alignment, your navigation system should be readily identifiable and easy to use (Niederst, 2001).

If you are using Web-design software to organize your portfolio, you will have the option of inserting a navigation element onto your Web pages. You will be given several options of how you want your pages to link. Good planning and organization come into play at this point. Once you have identified the major sections of your portfolio and arranged your artifacts accordingly, you can select the appropriate navigation system for your portfolio. If you are using other software, such as Microsoft Word, PowerPoint, or Publisher, you will need to design the navigational system yourself. Either way, make sure your audience can navigate to your main page and to every organizational page from anywhere in your portfolio.

Another way to make sure your audience keeps on track is to include a site index in your portfolio. A site index is nothing more than an index arranged in outline form with every entry hyperlinking to the corresponding page. This feature is not difficult to make and is appreciated by your viewer when she wants to refer to an artifact but forgets where she saw it, or if she wants to make sure she has examined all the artifacts in your portfolio.

Color

Color influences the look and feel of your portfolio. The use of color in conjunction with the element of contrast can create a page that is bold and dramatic or sophisticated and understated. If you are not careful, however, you might create a page that is difficult to read or one that is confusing and busy. Much of the success of your pages depends upon your use of color.

The element of color is a consideration in all of the parts of your page. The background, graphics, type, hyperlinks, and features such as sidebars and horizontal rules, all involve color. Making the right decisions involves experimentation and some basic knowledge of how color works in the electronic medium.

First, be aware that the best pages are designed using only a few colors. Investigate Web sites and you will quickly see the most visually pleasing sites use a limited color palette. If you decide to use soft colors with a subdued contrast, your page will look more sophisticated. If you use primary colors with a high degree of contrast, you will create a page that is bold and dramatic. Decide on the message or tone that you want your portfolio to convey and pick your colors accordingly. Whatever look you are going for, keep your palette of colors small to avoid visual confusion (Morris, 1999).

Backgrounds are an area that also need careful consideration. Visit Google™ and you will notice the clean look that comes from its white background. Of course, many other colors can work well, but you should be aware the color you select significantly influences your audience's perception of your site.

If you want to use a color, a soft pastel or neutral color works well. Subtle textures can also create a pleasing effect as long as they do not interfere with readability. Even some subtle graphics can be tiled to create a nice background. Often, however, backgrounds overpower the content of the page, making text difficult to read and distracting to the audience. Remember, the background is not the most important element on your page. It should not call attention to itself (Morris, 1999).

Another potential pitfall in selecting colors for your organizational pages is that, in spite of your best efforts, your portfolio may look different on someone else's computer. You cannot control how others set their browser options or their monitor settings. That lovely shade of lavender you used for your background might look like dried mud on your principal's monitor. Such problems are a fact of life in Web design.

The easiest way to avoid this problem is to use what designers call Web-safe or browser-safe colors. These are a collection of 216 colors that will look the same on virtually any computer. Web-safe colors are defined by the proportions of red, green, and blue that they contain. These proportions are known as the RGB values. If a color is Web-safe, its RGB values will be a combination of 00, 51, 102, 153, 204, or 255. Any other value for one of the three colors (red, green, or blue) means that the color is not Web-safe (Williams & Tollett, 2000). Web-safe colors are available in various Web design books and on the Web at sites such as, <www.visibone.com/colorlab/>.

If you think your audience may be using older equipment or may have their monitor options set to view a limited number of colors, then use Web-safe colors. Although this process may sound complex, it is not. Pick your Web-safe colors, enter their RGB values into the software program you are using, and you will have created your own custom color palette. Then, you can rest assured that the colors you are using are the same colors your audience will be viewing.

Graphics

Graphics add visual interest to your portfolio. They can be decorative or serve as artifacts to document your portfolio's objectives. One strength of an electronic portfolio is how easy it is to incorporate various media into one presentation, and graphics are easy to add. All you need to know are a few basics. Every graphic you incorporate into your portfolio will be either a GIF file or a JPG file. Each one has its particular characteristics and strengths.

GIF files are great to use when you have a graphic that is composed of flat colors with few gradations. Illustrations such as logos and cartoons are often GIF images. GIF files have several advantages. They are viewable on any computer platform, they are compressed, which means their file size is small and they will load quickly, and you can select one color in a GIF and make it transparent. You will want to use this technique if a graphic has a background color that is different from the background color of the page. If you make the background of the GIF transparent, the background color of the page will show through, and your graphic will not have a "pasted on" look (Figure 8.3).

Some images do not do well as GIFs, however. Photographs, such as those

Figure 8.3. Examples of a "pasted on" GIF and a GIF with a transparent background.

You will find that most clipart automatically inserts with a transparent background. However, some GIFs do not, and you will probably have to make the background transparent yourself. Use "Set Transparent Color" from the Picture toolbar.
GIF used by permission from Clips Ahoy! Free Clipart Island <http://www.clipsahoy.com/>.

you take with a digital camera, and other graphics that have many color gradations usually work better as JPG files. JPG files can take advantage of up to 16.7 million colors to create precise colors and shading that are not possible with GIF files. However, you cannot make any part of a JPG graphic transparent, so if you absolutely need transparency, you will have to save your graphic as a GIF file.

An advantage of JPG files is you can select the compression level you want to use in your photo editing software. The more you compress a JPG file, the smaller the file becomes, and the smaller the file size, the more quickly it will load. Compression has an effect on picture quality, however, so it is a good idea to experiment with a copy of your picture before you compress the file (Williams & Tollett, 2000).

Whether your graphics are GIF files, or JPG files or a combination of both, make sure you make the graphic the correct dimensions for your page before you save it. Save the file at 72 ppi (pixels per inch). For JPG files, save at the highest compression level you can without sacrificing too much quality. For GIF files, reduce the color palette to the fewest colors possible for the graphic. These steps will ensure the size of your graphic files is as small as possible so that your pages load quickly (Niederst, 2001).

Manipulating graphic files requires photo editing software. Some versions of Office come with Microsoft Photo Editor (look in Office Tools). Although it provides only the basics, Photo Editor works fine for resizing and compression. Adobe PhotoShop is generally regarded as the premier photo editing software, but it comes with a fairly hefty price tag. PhotoShop Elements is less expensive and has many of the advanced features found in the full version. If you have a different photo editing program with the necessary features, there is no reason not to use it.

While constructing your portfolio you may encounter another type of graphics file, the TIFF file. TIFF files are typically created by scanning software and are an option in photo editing software and graphics programs. If you find you have graphics in TIFF format, you should convert them to GIF or JPG files. Try not to use TIFF files in your portfolio, as they are much larger than either GIF or JPG files; they will take up much more space and cause your portfolio to load more slowly.

Type

Readability is the most important factor to consider when selecting the font for your portfolio. Readability affects the style you select, the number of styles you use, size of the type, and layout of the text. Making good decisions regarding type will result in attractive, readable pages, while errors in judgment will make your portfolio unattractive and hard to read.

Conventional wisdom advises that you use no more than two type styles per page. Of course, you want your finished portfolio to develop as a unified whole, so you should repeat the same one or two fonts throughout your organizational pages. Although most print publications rely on a serif font for text (a font with little feet) and a sans serif font (without the feet) for titles and headlines, the opposite is true for type viewed on a screen. A clean sans serif font like Arial is a good choice for text. Set titles in a serif font such as, Times New Roman (Morris, 1999).

You should limit your choices to standard fonts if you are publishing to the Web because you cannot control your audience's browser settings. If you set your Web portfolio in type that is not supported by your audience's browser, it will convert the type to something else. That something else may make your pages hard to read or unattractive. It is better to stick with type styles you can be fairly sure will appear the way you intend.

Another factor to consider when selecting type is the size you will use for text and headings. Again, these should be consistent, or at least fairly so, among your organizational pages. Type set smaller than 10 points is usually too small to read easily, while type larger than 12 or 14 looks amateurish. Headings and titles should be set in a size that works well with the size of text and layout of the page. Use the element of proximity to keep headings close to their related text (Williams & Tollett, 2000).

Make sure the color of your text contrasts well with your background, headings, and titles. Black type on a white background or white type on a black background are considered traditional choices. However, you should feel free to select your own color scheme as long as readability does not suffer. When considering colors, do not forget the colors of your hyperlinks. These also need to be readable also. Furthermore, the color should harmonize well with the surrounding text.

Finally, you should consider the layout of your pages. If you are including large blocks of text, consider putting the text in columns, similar to magazine or newspaper pages. Text is easier to read in this format, especially on a computer screen, and will increase your portfolio's readability.

Good and Bad Design

Bringing all the elements of good design together can seem overwhelming,

Figure 8.4. An example of bad layout and design.

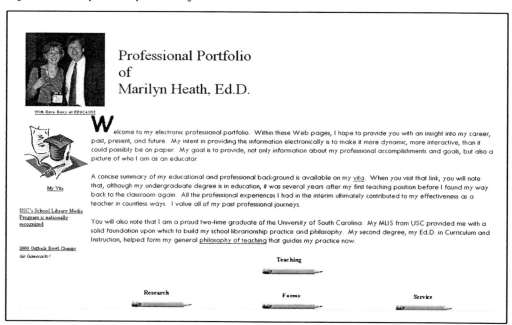

There are many reasons to criticize my first attempt at an electronic portfolio. The page looks cluttered and unorganized because of poor layout and mixed alignments. I did not effectively use the white space to create proximity between elements that belong together. The navigation graphics did provide repetition throughout the portfolio, but they are obtrusive. The choice of type fonts is good, although the text is so small that it is hard to read. I also did not reduce the file size of my graphics before inserting them, which made them load slowly, and I originally used two logos without checking to see if I needed permission.

but it does not have to be. Problems start to crop up when you have more ambition than experience. If you are a neophyte, then keep your plans modest. You will find good design, because of its emphasis on repetition, unity, and organization, will actually make your portfolio project much easier to accomplish. Simplicity should be your watchword.

Figure 8.5. An example of good portfolio layout and design.

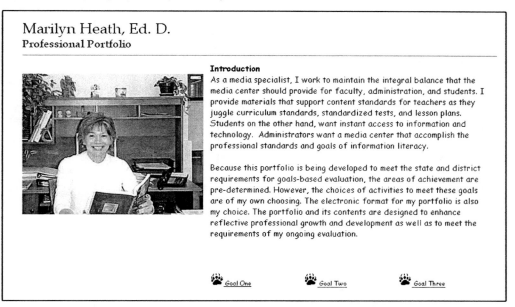

This portfolio is much better than its predecessor. Notice the strong vertical and horizontal alignment. Type styles and colors are kept at a minimum. There is a definite hierarchy of elements on the page. The navigation element is easy to find but not obtrusive.

Look back over the sample portfolio pages in the previous chapter. Although they were designed with different programs, they have one thing in common: good layout and design. If you still need convincing, take a look at the sample pages in Figures 8.4 and 8.5. Figure 8.4 was my first attempt at portfolio design and my first project with Microsoft FrontPage. It looks busy, unorganized, and confusing. (I was busy, unorganized, and confused.) The viewer has no idea what to look at first. Compare it to the page in Figure 8.5. Notice how clean and organized this page looks and how natural it is for the eye to move from the picture to the accompanying text. This page is more effective because it follows the basics of good design and illustrates the maxim less is more. You can achieve the results you want with a knowledge of design basics, a good layout, and some practice (Figure 8.6).

Summary

Once you have chosen the organizational software for your portfolio, it is a good idea to experiment with it. Make sure you familiarize yourself with its features, especially those that pertain to developing your portfolio. Then, use the features to try your hand at combining the elements of good design.

First, experiment with the organization of your portfolio. If you are using

Figure 8.6. An example of an electronic portfolio main page, objective page, and artifact page.

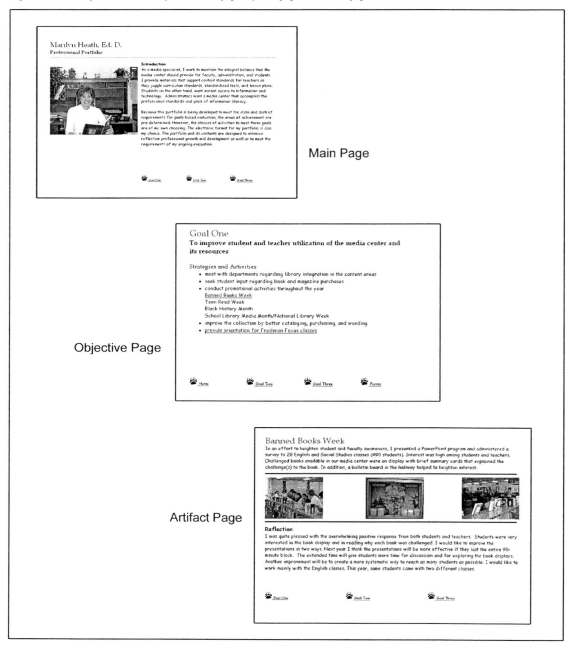

These pages were created in Microsoft FrontPage and then saved to a CD-ROM instead of published to the Web. Notice the uniformity created by repetition of key design elements, such as color, type style, alignment, and navigation. Repetition makes it easy to tell that the pages belong together even though they do not look exactly the same.

Web software, you will have access to a navigation feature that lets you build your Web site and organize it as you go. If you haven't already done so, make sure that all of your artifacts and reflections are organized by objective so you can find them easily as you build your portfolio. Then, use good Web development techniques: Name your files so they are easily recognizable. Keep file names short, replace spaces between words with underscores, and eliminate symbols. It is also a good idea to place all graphics in a separate folder. This will make them easy to find.

Once you have decided on the structure of your portfolio, experiment with the layout of your portfolio pages. Remember, you are designing for a horizontal space, not a vertical one as you would with paper. Try to keep the content of your organization pages contained to one or two screens. Your main page should be no larger than one screen with no scrolling.

As you experiment with the design of your pages, keep in mind you should probably use a flush left alignment to keep your page elements organized. This alignment will help give your pages a clean, orderly look and make them easy for your audience to navigate. Used in conjunction with alignment, proximity can also help organize your page by using space to separate page elements. Try grouping the information on your pages to gauge the effect proximity has on your page design.

Another design technique that groups elements on a page is the use of contrast. By choosing a focal point and then establishing a hierarchy of the remaining page elements, you establish an order of importance, which also helps to organize the page. Contrast can be bold and dramatic or soft and subtle; what you choose depends on the purpose of the page and the message you intend to convey.

Repetition is the technique that brings unity to all of the pages of your portfolio. By using repetition in your colors, layout, spacing, fonts, and other page elements, you tie your pages together to create a unified whole. Without repetition, your portfolio pages will appear unconnected. Experiment with your own choices of color, background, font, and layout, create cascading style sheets, or select a predesigned theme in your organizational software.

Another design element that requires your attention is the design of your navigation system. If you are using Web development software, you can automatically insert your navigation hyperlinks on every page. Otherwise, you will need to construct your links and insert them yourself. In either case, your navigation must remain consistent from one page to another, both in appearance and in placement. Your user should always be able to return to the organizational pages from anywhere in your portfolio. Also, consider adding a site index to your portfolio so users can easily find and link to a particular page.

Color is an important design element for you to consider. Color will do much to set the tone and message of your portfolio. You must carefully select the color of your background, type, graphics, and other elements, such as sidebars, lines, and borders. Often, people make the mistake of using too many colors or using backgrounds that are too busy. Always keep in mind your content is the most important element of your portfolio; everything else should enhance it, not overpower it or distract from it. You also need to keep in mind, if you plan on publishing your portfolio on the Web, you should use Web-safe colors so your portfolio will appear as you intend.

In designing your portfolio pages, take care when choosing font styles. One or two are sufficient, with the text of your portfolio set in a sans serif font, such as Arial, and headings and titles set in a serif font, such as Times New Roman. Experiment with type size, proximity of headings, and columns to make your portfolio as readable as possible.

Finally, be sure to include graphics in your portfolio for visual interest. Know when to use GIF files and when JPG files are appropriate and how to make each as small as possible. You will need a photo editing program such as Adobe

PhotoShop for sophisticated photo editing, but for simple procedures there are several software programs that will work well.

Design is an art, and you will need practice to gain confidence and skill. Don't be afraid to experiment and ask others for their opinions as you make design decisions. If you anticipate developing a substantial portfolio or several portfolios in the coming years, or if you are interested in learning more about design concepts and how to apply them, the book *The Non-Designer's Web Book* (Williams & Tollett, 2000) is an invaluable tool.

Chapter Nine
Sharing your Professional Portfolio

No matter what the purpose of your portfolio, you will find the process of creating it is an invaluable professional growth experience. As you collect, select, and critically consider your artifacts, you will delve into your professional life in a way you never have before. Writing reflections for each of your pieces helps you recognize your thoughts, beliefs, and dispositions; you will come to a richer and fuller understanding of yourself as an educator.

If you have collaborated with colleagues during this process, so much the better. It is helpful to share the experience with others who are also developing portfolios. Whether you schedule regular work sessions or share experiences in the hallway between classes, it helps to be able to share in the successes, concerns, inspirations, and pitfalls of a fellow portfolio developer. (Anyone who has undergone the National Board certification process knows this to be true.) There is a dynamic among colleagues that adds another dimension and makes the experience more enriching.

It is always helpful to have another perspective of your work. Seeing what you do through the eyes of others can reveal a new meaning to your practice. When you develop your portfolio, share it with others. In the process, you may gain valuable input to incorporate into your portfolio.

Sharing your portfolio with others can open avenues of communication that lead to valuable exchanges. You may inspire others to develop portfolios. Possibly a colleague will want to collaborate with you on a lesson. Students may see what happens in the classroom in a new light or offer valuable insights from their perspective. Administrators will appreciate your efforts and initiative to grow professionally. Sharing is a way to validate that what you have done is meaningful and worthwhile; sharing helps to validate not just your portfolio, but also the career that it represents.

Sharing with Colleagues

It is important to share your portfolio with your colleagues as you develop it. Ideally, a group of you will develop your portfolios at the same time and meet periodically. It is often helpful to discuss various problems encountered in the development process and to share strategies, tips, and successes. An important element in this process is to review each other's work to offer support, suggestions, and direction.

Sharing the development of our portfolios with peers can be risky business. When we share personal information with others, we become vulnerable. We allow ourselves to be open to indifference or criticism. By being open with our colleagues, however, we are inviting them to build an open relationship—one that is conducive to sharing and learning. Such relationships can have a powerful effect on each of us as learners and as educators.

Sharing the portfolio development process with our peers holds us accountable. Creating a professional portfolio can be a difficult, time-consuming process. Because it is intensely personal, it can also be an isolating experience if we let it. However, if we have made the commitment with others, then we have a responsibility, not only to ourselves, but to our group. Even a group of two or three can become a learning community that sustains each other.

Perhaps you and a few colleagues have decided to create professional development portfolios as an alternative to district offerings. You have a desire for authentic professional development—learning and growing in ways that matter to you. Each of you embarks on your portfolio development journey, and in the process, discovers you share many common goals and objectives for future development. You make a commitment to reach these goals together, and you become closer, both personally and professionally. This process encourages the development of valuable professional associations that can lead to mutual lifelong learning.

"Personal reflection feeds and is enriched by a learning community" (Grant, 1996).

Although you may not notice at first, what you do has an impact on others in your workplace. If you and your small group develop portfolios together, other teachers will take note. Share with them what you are doing and why. No matter the purpose of your portfolio, you can share the virtues of portfolio development and its relationship to reflection and personal professional knowledge. You can share your knowledge of the portfolio development process and offer to act as a portfolio development mentor.

After you have completed your portfolio, share it with others in your school or district. Possibly, those in your department would be interested in what you have developed. You may be able to offer a brief question-and-answer session during a faculty meeting or a staff development day. You could write an article for the school or district newsletter and include your portfolio's Web address. Teaching can be an isolating profession, but often, if we make the effort and have the courage to openly share with our colleagues, we are pleasantly surprised to find that others are interested in what we have done because they share our concerns, hopes, and goals.

Sharing with Students

Sharing our portfolio development process with students can give us another perspective on our pedagogy. Although it may not be appropriate to divulge a résumé portfolio to students, their input can be invaluable for a showcase, evaluation, or professional development portfolio. In higher education, it is standard practice to ask students to evaluate their classes each semester. However, in the elementary and secondary grades students do not always get a chance to share their assessments of class work. Asking students to participate in evaluating their learning experiences will also help them be more active participants and can help create a collaborative learning community within the classroom.

Another benefit of including student input in the portfolio development process is to strengthen and enhance your position as a role model or mentor. When your students see that you value learning, that learning is a process not an accomplishment, and that you continually strive for a higher degree of mastery of your profession, you set a powerful example. Sharing your experience and accomplishments helps them recognize and appreciate your professionalism.

Sharing with Administrators

Another good source of input for your professional portfolio is your principal, assistant principal, or district office personnel. If you are developing an evaluation portfolio, then the appropriate administrator will surely have ongoing contributions in the evaluation process. Sharing your portfolio as you go will help you do a better job of meeting your evaluation requirements and keep your administrator abreast of your evaluation efforts.

If you are developing a showcase or professional development portfolio, you can also benefit from administrative input, whether in the form of classroom observations or reactions to your reflections. An administrator's perspective can help you recognize both strengths and weaknesses in your practice as well as reinforce self-evaluations you have already made. If you are a pre-service teacher, you have the additional resource of your practice teaching supervisor to contribute yet another perspective of your work.

Sharing with Your Audience

Ultimately, your goal is to share your portfolio with the audience for whom it is intended. Depending upon your needs and desires, you will publish your portfolio to the Web or copy and distribute it via a floppy disk, a Zip disk, or a CD-ROM. Either method involves special publication considerations as well as the legal considerations associated with copyright law and use of trademarks.

Publishing to the Web

If you have chosen to publish your portfolio on the Web, then you will have some special concerns to consider. Your first consideration is to find an Internet Service Provider (ISP) where you can publish your portfolio. There are several possibilities for free server space, including your personal ISP and the district server. If neither of these is suitable, an online search at sites such as <www.freewebspace.com> may locate other possibilities. If you need more server space than is available for free, then you will have to purchase space. Again, your personal ISP is a good place to start, but other Internet sites are available as well. Many offer Web space at modest prices.

If you will allow unrestricted access to your portfolio, then you do not need to be concerned about privacy issues. However, make sure you do not include personal information such as Social Security number, home address, or phone number. If you require a password to access your Web site, then make sure you distribute that information promptly and accurately to only those persons who are your intended audience.

When you are ready to publish your Web site, you will need to upload it to the appropriate server. This action involves using file transfer protocol (FTP) software such as WS_FTP. A trial version of this program is available for you to download at no charge from <www.wsftp.com>. You can also search the Internet for other free FTP software if you prefer. Once you have the FTP software on your computer, it is a simple matter of selecting the folder that contains your portfolio and transferring it to the server. You will need to know the path name on the server where your portfolio will reside. You can get this information from the company whose server is providing you with space. If you used Microsoft FrontPage or Dreamweaver to produce your portfolio, these programs provide upload capabilities so that other FTP software is unnecessary. No matter how you upload your portfolio, make sure you have included every file. Take care to check all graphics, audio, and video files are present so your portfolio is complete, all links active, and all media files loading.

Publishing to a Disk

If you have chosen to publish your portfolio on a disk, you will not be as concerned with privacy and security issues. You will, however, have other concerns. The first and overriding consideration is that the software you have used to create your portfolio must be available on the viewer's computer for your portfolio to open and work properly. If you used programs such as Microsoft Word, PowerPoint, Publisher, Excel, and HyperStudio, your viewers must have the same programs installed on their computers. **You must be certain your viewers have access to the software programs you used to create your portfolio or your portfolio will not open on their computers.** If you have PDF files you converted in Adobe Acrobat, then your audience must have the free download of Adobe Reader installed. If you are not sure, you might consider providing a hyperlink to the Web site. If you have used Web development software, such as Microsoft FrontPage or

Figure 9.1. Comparison of storage media used for electronic portfolios.

Type of Disk	Capacity	Strengths/Weaknesses
Floppy Disk	1.44 MB	Readily available and easy to use/Small storage capacity
Zip Disk	100 MB, 250 MB, 750 MB	Large storage capacity, easy to use, rewriteable/ Drives not always available, drives are backwards-compatible only*; not widely used, expensive
CD-ROM	700 MB	Easy to use, drives readily available, read-only, inexpensive/ Cannot be edited unless the disk is CD-ROMRW
Memory Key	16 MB to 256 MB	Portability, compatibility/ Relatively expensive

*Newer 750 MB Zip drives will read that size disk plus the smaller 250 MB and 100 MB disks. Similarly, the 250 MB drive will read that disk and the 100 MB disk. However, the drives do not have the capability of reading a larger disk. For example, a 100 MB drive cannot read a 250 MB or a 750 MB disk.

Dreamweaver, your portfolio will open in Internet Explorer or Netscape Navigator even if you have published it on a disk.

As you select the best medium for publishing, consider the size of your final portfolio. Basically, you have four options: a floppy disk, a Zip disk, a CD-ROM, or a memory key. A floppy disk is acceptable for only the most basic portfolio. Although it has the advantages of familiarity, availability, and economy, its small capacity makes it unusable in most instances (Figure 9.1). Zip disks, on the other hand, have a much larger capacity and have the advantage that they can be edited and reused as your portfolio evolves over time. Zip drives, however, are not as popular as floppy and CD-ROM drives, so you will have to be sure your audience has this hardware before you decide to use this storage device. Zip disks remain fairly expensive compared to most other portable media.

CD-ROM drives are nearly as ubiquitous as floppy drives, so you can avert the accessibility issue if you choose to publish to a CD-ROM. Another asset of CD-ROMs is their larger capacity. Unless you invest in CD-ROMRW (rewriteable) disks, you will not be able to edit your original disk, but will have to burn a new copy each time you make a change to your portfolio. Given the low cost of disks, this is probably not an issue. In fact, this feature may be an asset because your audience cannot unintentionally alter or delete any part of your portfolio, which might happen with a floppy disk or Zip disk.

Whichever disk you select, you will want to make sure that it has a professional-looking label. You can purchase label-making kits for CD-ROMs and printable labels that will fit floppy disks and Zip disks. When you label your disk, you should include your name, the type of portfolio, and any instructions for opening it. Contact information is also helpful if you have room. Otherwise, make sure that contact information is included within your portfolio.

The newest type of storage medium is commonly known as a memory key and goes by various brand names. A small storage device about the size of a key, plugs into a computer's USB slot. Memory keys come in a variety of capacities from 16MB to 256 MB, so you can purchase the one that fits your needs. Memory keys are rewritable and can be used on virtually any machine that has a USB port. At this time they are still relatively expensive, and there is no good way to label them. As with most electronic innovations, prices will likely decrease over time, making them more feasible for portfolio storage.

Legal Issues

Legal issues are probably the most overlooked aspect of portfolio development. Generally, infringement of copyright and trademark violations are the two legal issues that pertain to portfolio development. Because most of the content of your portfolio is your own work or reflections, these issues may not pertain to your portfolio at all because you have control over your own work and can do with it what you please. However, it is possible, and maybe even likely, that you have included examples of student work, pictures of students, graphics you downloaded, or trademark symbols.

If so, then you will need to obtain permission from those parties to use their work or their images in your portfolio. You should obtain permission from a parent or guardian to use student work, if the student is under 18, or the image of any student who is recognizable in a photo. The permission form should state the purpose of your portfolio and how the person's work or image will be used in the portfolio. It is likely your district already has a standard permission form that you can use. It is a good idea to obtain these permissions during the portfolio development process so you do not run into any unexpected problems as you near completion. Even when permission is granted, do not publish students' full names or other information that might compromise their privacy and security.

Some other common pitfalls to avoid are related to trademarks. Using trademarks without attribution is a common mistake many Web page creators make. Often, this is done to provide a hyperlink from one page to another. For example, you may want to provide your audience with a hyperlink to a program they need to download to access one of your documents. It is not necessary for you to request permission to provide a word link or a URL, but if you use the company's trademark or logo, you must have permission to use it as a hyperlink. Some Web sites, such as Adobe, encourage using the small logo and provide a button that has the link embedded just for that purpose. However, any time you use a trademark (such as "Xerox" in place of "photocopy") you will want to put the trademark symbol (^{TM}) as the last character of the trademark. In Word you can find the trademark symbol by pulling down the Insert menu, selecting Symbol, and clicking on the Special Characters tab. You can also use the keyboard shortcut: ctr-alt-t.

Click-wrap agreements are another area that can cause potential problems. A click-wrap agreement usually accompanies items such as clip art, shareware, freeware, or other material that may be labeled "royalty-free." Usually, before you can download this material, you are given terms and conditions to which you agree by clicking on the "I Accept" button. It is important to read the terms and conditions and then use the downloaded material appropriately so as not to be in violation of the agreement you have made. Some material can be used in print products, but may not be used online so using it in a portfolio you intend to publish on the Web could be a violation of the agreement.

Copyright and Fair Use

Most educators are familiar with the term "fair use" even if they are not sure what it means. Unfortunately, some teachers mistakenly think it means they have permission to copy and use anything they want for their classrooms as long as it is for educational purposes. Such thinking is misguided and can lead to abuses of the fair use principle. When multimedia production, Web access and publication are added to the context of fair use, the issue can get even cloudier. Although there is no single, simple test to determine fair use, there are several general principles that should guide educators as they produce and publish their electronic portfolios.

First, you should be clear as to the meanings of both copyright and fair use. Basically, copyright is a property right that grants a creator such as an author, artist, or composer, exclusive rights to his or her original work and derivatives thereof. The owner of the work has control over any type of reproduction, distribution, or production. Copyright law is commonly associated with printed material, but also includes music, dramatic works, pictures, graphics, sculpture, motion pictures, audiovisual works, and sound recordings. To qualify for copyright, a work must be original, creative, and in a fixed or tangible form of expression (Newsome 1997).

It is a misconception creators have to apply for copyright protection; since 1978 works are protected as soon as they take a tangible form. The owner does not have to apply for copyright, and a copyright notice does not have to be attached. Anything that was protected by copyright as of the enactment date of the Sonny Bono Copyright Term Extension Act (CTEA) of 1998 is protected for 70 years beyond the life of the author(s), or 95 years from the date of creation for a corporate work such as a motion picture. However, many works copyrighted prior to 1978 are now in the public domain because of errors in registration, failure to renew, or lack of initial registration of the (then required) notice. If you are using more of a work originally copyrighted before 1978 than is allowed under fair use, you will need to do a thorough analysis of the copyright situation to determine if it is protected or in the public domain. Other works in the public domain include U.S. government documents (state, county, city, and other government documents may or may not be protected by copyright) and may also be used without permission (Simpson, 2001).

Under most circumstances, permission must be received from the copyright owner to use a copyrighted work. However, copyright law identifies the concept of fair use and provides four tests to determine if the fair use exemption is applicable. These standards address the purpose of the use, the nature of the work, the proportion or extent of the material used, and the effect the use may have on the work's marketability or the value of the work. In addition, multimedia productions created by educators must comply with specific multimedia guidelines. First, this means that the production must be used for instruction. Educators may then retain the production for a limited time to use for peer conferences or for inclusion in their professional portfolios. The allowable extent of material used is similar to fair use principles applied to print materials (Figure 9.2).

Figure 9.2. Fair use guidelines for copyrighted work used in multimedia productions.

Medium	Extent Allowed
Video	10% or 3 minutes, whichever is less
Text	1000 words or 10%, whichever is less
Poems – 250 words or less	In its entirety, but no more than three poems per author
Poems – more than 250 words	Excerpt no longer than 250 words; three excerpts per poet or five excerpts per anthology
Music and Lyrics	10%, but no longer than 30 seconds
Photographs and Illustrations	10% or 15 images from a collected work, whichever is less; no more than 5 images per artist or photographer
Numerical Data	10% or 2500 fields or cell entries, whichever is less

Guidelines developed by the Conference on Fair Use, 1996.

The multimedia guidelines specify restrictions other than extent of material used. First, is the time restriction. Educational multimedia projects used for instruction may be retained for two years from the initial presentation. Use after that time requires permission for each copyrighted item used. There are also limitations on copying and distribution. No more than two copies of the presentation may be made in addition to the one original, but if a group of teachers works together to create a project, each may have a copy. In addition, multimedia projects containing copyrighted material may not be published over electronic networks without permission unless the network is secure. (See the guidelines for a definition of "secure".) If the network access is not secure, the work may be posted for 14 days. After 14 days the work may be put on reserve, but specific instructions not to copy must be made if checking out the reserve copy.

Furthermore, it is your responsibility to credit each source of copyrighted material in your production and to include a notice that certain materials are copyrighted and are restricted from further use. If you use multimedia presentations that include copyrighted materials for instructional purposes, you would be wise to consult a detailed, authoritative source, such as Simpson's *Copyright for Schools: A Practical Guide* (2001).

What does all of this mean in terms of your electronic portfolio? First, your professional portfolio does not qualify for the educational fair use exemption because it is not created for instructional use. Therefore, if you plan to include copyrighted materials beyond what is allowable under the fair use tests, you must ask for and receive permission for use and display the appropriate copyright notices. Even if your portfolio includes copyrighted material you used for instructional purposes, the purpose of the portfolio in which that material now resides is not instructional. Even if you did not originally have to ask for permission under the fair use guidelines, you would now have to receive permission and include appropriate notices to use the material in your portfolio.

Remember, any material you use that you did not create may be protected by copyright. If it was created since 1978, the owner did not have to apply for copyright for the work to be protected. Also, the copyright symbol or notice does not have to be displayed on copyrighted works, so the lack of a © symbol does not mean the work is free for the taking. If you are in doubt whether a work is protected or not, err on the side of caution and assume it is. If it appears you will need several trademark or copyright permissions, you may want to consult a reference that specializes in these matters. A good one is *Getting Permission: How to License & Clear Copyrighted Materials Online & Off* (Stim, 2001).

There are two simple ways to avoid any confusion and potential legal problems. The first is not to use any copyrighted material in your portfolio that exceeds the fair use tests. Usually, this is the easiest way to avoid problems. Since your portfolio primarily contains material originally created by you, the issue of copyright may not pertain to your portfolio at all. The other way to avoid problems is to ask for and receive permission for each work you use. If you use anyone else's work, including that of your students, make sure you ask for and receive permission as necessary. Be careful to check your portfolio's contents, especially graphics, and ask for permission even if you originally used an item under fair use and/or are unsure if it is copyrighted. With permission, you may then publish and copy your portfolio with the confidence you are abiding by copyright law.

Summary

Sharing your professional portfolio should not begin with the final product. In order to make your portfolio as effective as it can be, you should begin sharing the process early on. Sharing with colleagues is an especially effective strategy for good portfolio development. Collaboration can be structured or informal and as involved as you want it to be. The idea is to bring other perspectives, observations, and assessments of your practice to the portfolio development process.

For these reasons, it is also helpful to share your portfolio with students. Not only will their input be helpful and enlightening, but you will be identifying yourself as a learner—a professional who values learning, growing, achieving, and improving. Your administrators can also help you by offering yet another perspective and by being involved in the development process. Such involvement, especially with an evaluation portfolio, will help you improve your portfolio and make your evaluation process more instructive and meaningful.

As you approach the final stages of portfolio development, you will either be publishing your portfolio to the Web or copying it on disks for distribution. There are several considerations for either method of publication, including the size of your portfolio, privacy and security concerns, and legal issues. It is important to consider each of these issues carefully before publication is complete.

Chapter Ten
Putting It All Together

When you made the decision to develop an electronic professional portfolio, you committed yourself to develop an instrument that would fulfill a specific purpose. You wanted a portfolio you could use as a résumé, a showcase of your work, an evaluation instrument, or a tool for professional development. Beyond that, you recognized the need for a dynamic instrument—something more than a traditional résumé or standard evaluation form—that would display your knowledge, skills, dispositions, and professional growth. You wanted something uniquely personal, and you wanted to be able to choose the artifacts that you felt represent you best.

Your portfolio fulfills all of those requirements and more. You have discovered, by now, that the process of portfolio development is also an intense learning experience. You have learned about your pedagogy as you currently practice it: you have learned about your strengths and weaknesses, what you believe and how it influences your practice, and how others assess what you do. You have also looked ahead to make decisions about what you want to learn and how you want to grow. You have set goals and objectives. You have a plan for the future. You have become a student of your own practice.

> ". . . something wonderful occurs when teachers are involved in the learning processes required to create digital teaching portfolios—teachers get the chance to become learners" (Kilbane & Milman, 2003, p. 23).

You have also developed some new technology skills along the way. Maybe, you acquired a new piece of equipment or a new software program. If so, you are probably proficient with its use by now. Possibly, you have learned to use existing equipment and software in new ways. In either case, you know more than you did when you started; an achievement that might possibly add another dimension to your pedagogy.

At this point, you have put many hours of thought, planning, and work into the development of your electronic portfolio. When you finish that final entry, it is tempting to sit back, wipe your brow, and say, "Whew, I'm glad that's over!" However, it would be a shame to do all this work only to find you have overlooked some factor that makes your portfolio less than it should be. Take some time to review the portfolio development process and then conduct a final check.

Professional Portfolio Development in a Nutshell

- *Identify your purpose, goal, and objectives.* A portfolio without a purpose will not accomplish much. As you consider the various aspects of portfolio development, start with the specific reason you want to develop a portfolio and the accompanying goal you want your portfolio to help you achieve. Then develop objectives that support your goal. Make sure your objectives include your knowledge, skills, dispositions, and growth so that all aspects of your professional practice will be demonstrated in your portfolio. As you attend to development issues, also consider the audience of your portfolio and whether they may have particular needs or restrictions regarding electronic portfolios. Begin to consider any specific requirements your portfolio may present, whether in its organization or with the hardware or software used for development.

- *Create a working portfolio.* Creating a working portfolio is a two-step process. First, you need to answer the question, "What did I do?" in the context of your portfolio's goal and objectives. To do so involves collecting artifacts that document the knowledge, skills, dispositions, and growth articulated in your objectives. After you have collected everything that might possibly be included in your portfolio, it is time to move to the second phase: selection. Selection involves examining your collected artifacts and answering the question, "What did I do best?" There are several criteria to use in making this judgment, including professional standards, how closely aligned the artifact is with your objectives, how many of your objectives the artifact supports, and the variety of artifacts in your selection. As you work, you will organize your artifacts according to the objective or other organizing element they support. You may need to repeat the selection process more than once to finally arrive at a collection of artifacts that will be included in your portfolio.

- *Reflect on each artifact.* Now it is time to answer the question, "What did I learn?" Formulating a response involves the process of reflection; the heart of professional development. Reflection links your practice to professional knowledge, examines your beliefs and assumptions, and ultimately leads to professional growth. Reflection leads to self-knowledge and can be accomplished by a variety of activities, including journal writing, professional conversations, and observations. When you reflect for your portfolio, you need to consider the artifact in the context of the instructional setting. Think about what went right and what went wrong. Did it meet the learning needs of all your students? How does it relate to professional standards or your instructional goals? Answering these and related questions will help you fully understand what you learned from the activity or event the artifact represents.

- *Plan for the future.* Reflecting upon and understanding your present pedagogy will help you plan for the future. By considering the question, "What will I do next?" you use knowledge of your current practice to construct new understandings of what you do. As you consider an activity's strengths and weaknesses, you can plan to affect changes. You might alter a particular lesson or incorporate a change that influences your entire pedagogy. Change involves planning; reflecting on specific artifacts can lead you to a broader focus that helps you formulate goals and objectives for future professional growth.

- *Make hardware and software decisions.* Now that the content of your portfolio is ready, it is time to begin production. The first step is to make hardware and software decisions. What you choose to use will depend upon your expertise, what is available, and what, if any, new technology skills you want to acquire. You also need to take into account the needs or requirements of your audience. Web design software is a first choice for portfolio development because its purpose is to design content to be viewed on a computer screen. Also, it offers many features and options not available in some other programs. Other programs can work well also, and the important aspect is your expertise with the software you select. Various hardware considerations also have to be taken into account. You must have a computer capable of supporting the software you select. You will probably need to have access to and know how to use a scanner. A digital camera is also a handy item, but is not absolutely necessary, especially if you can scan prints.

- *Follow good principles of design.* As you develop your portfolio, pay particular attention to the elements of design. Your portfolio should be structured in an orderly, logical way that is easy to navigate. Individual "pages" should have a layout that is organized and easy to follow. As much as possible, pages should include very little vertical scrolling with no horizontal scrolling whatsoever. Organize your pages by the effectual use of space and unify your portfolio through the repetition of background, type styles, fonts, layout, and color. Make sure the navigation element lets your viewer get where she wants to go. Understand the basic properties of graphics and how to use them.

- *Share your portfolio with others.* Sharing your portfolio during the development process can be an enriching experience, especially if your colleagues are developing portfolios too. Sharing creates a community of support and helps make you accountable for the progress you make. Sharing can foster mutual learning and valuable professional friendships. Beyond sharing with colleagues, it is helpful to get perspectives from other people you work with. Administrators, who are familiar with standards and competencies, can help you identify areas for growth. Students, too, can bring a fresh perspective to your self-knowledge. Ask for their feedback and value their opinions.

- *Check for possible copyright and trademark problems.* If you are using material that was created by another person beyond what is allowed by fair use, you must ask permission. If you and another teacher collaborated on a lesson and you are using those materials, ask permission. If you are using photographs of others, ask their permission. Make sure you have permission from parents or other caregivers to use students' photographs and class work in your portfolio. Even if you do not identify the students in a picture, if they are recognizable, you need to ask permission. Do not assume that removing a student's name makes it all right to use their work; it does not, unless you have permission. When you ask for permission, clearly specify what you want to use, how you will use it, and why. Never identify a student by more than a first name, and do not provide any other private information such as addresses, phone numbers, or birthdays. Be aware educational fair use does not cover professional portfolios, so make sure you ask for and receive appropriate permissions. Follow the fair use guidelines that govern multimedia projects. Check carefully that you do not infringe on any trademarks, and be sure to abide by any click-wrap agreements for graphics or other materials.

- *Double check your portfolio prior to publication.* At this point make sure your portfolio looks the way you intend and that there are no errors. It is a good idea for someone else to "test drive" your portfolio to verify the organization is logical and easy to navigate. Make sure the layout and design elements on all organizational pages are the same. Do not overlook the little things: check spelling, grammar, and punctuation. Make sure all graphics load quickly. Check all hyperlinks and navigation elements; a broken link can undermine your hard work. If you are using copyrighted materials or trademarks, make sure you have included the appropriate symbols and permission statements.

- *Publish your portfolio to disk or to the Web.* If you are publishing to a disk, copy your portfolio to the appropriate storage medium—floppy, CD-ROM, Zip disk, or memory key—and make as many copies as you need. Label the disks with your name and contact information and include any necessary start-up instructions. If you are publishing your portfolio to the Web, upload your pages using the Upload command in the Web design software or by using FTP software. Before you upload, use the "preview in browser" feature to discover any flaws. After you publish your portfolio, go online and check your portfolio again. Provide the URL to your audience along with access information if the site is secure.

A Final Check

You have gone through the portfolio development process again and checked to make sure you did everything you were supposed to do. Now take time to look at your professional portfolio with a critical eye. Make sure your portfolio does what you intend and does it well. You may find the rubric in Appendix E helpful for evaluating your effort.

Summary

Now you are done. You have developed and published your professional portfolio, a record of your knowledge, skills, dispositions, and growth. It documents your best practice and functions as a showcase for your technology skills. It acts as a vehicle that allows you to examine your practice and to plan for future professional development. By creating this portfolio, you have crafted a rich, dynamic portrayal of your professional life while enhancing your image as a professional and an innovator. The portfolio development process has engaged you in reflection that fosters self-assessment and growth, the purpose of any authentic professional development activity. By examining and reflecting on your

"A teacher's portfolio enables us to do exactly what we ask our students to do: self-assess, self-evaluate, and self-regulate" (Van Wagenen & Hibbard, 1998, p. 29).

experiences, you have discovered the means to grow beyond them.

Remember, you have a goal and objectives for future professional growth so your journey is really just beginning. As you continue your career and professional development, use your portfolio to record and enhance your growth. Your portfolio, regardless of its purpose, is not only a collection of artifacts but is the ultimate artifact of your professional journey.

Portfolio Development Worksheet

Purpose: The purpose of my portfolio is _____

_____

Submission Requirements or Position Requirements: _____

_____

_____

_____

Applicable Professional Standards: _____

_____

_____

_____

Goal: The goal of my portfolio is _____

_____

Objectives:

My portfolio will demonstrate that _____

_____

My portfolio will demonstrate that _____

_____

My portfolio will demonstrate that _____

_____

√	Artifact Type	Objective #1	Objective #2	Objective #3
	Artifact Checklist			

√	Artifact Type	Objective #1	Objective #2	Objective #3
	Anecdotal Records			
	Assessments			
	Awards and Certificates			
	Bulletin Board Ideas			
	Case Studies			
	Classroom Management Philosophy & Strategies			
	Committees			
	Cooperative Learning Strategies			
	Curriculum Plans			
	Essays			
	Evaluations			
	Field Trip Plans			
	Floor Plans			
	Goal Statements			
	Individualized Plans			
	Interviews with Students, Teachers, Parents			
	Journals			
	Lesson Plans			
	Letters to Parents			
	Management and Organization Strategies			
	Media Competencies			
	Meetings and Workshops Log			
	Observation Reports			
	Peer Critiques			
	Philosophy Statement			
	Pictures and Photographs			
	Position Papers			
	Problem-Solving Logs			
	Professional Development Activities			
	Professional Affiliations			
	Professional Readings List			
	Projects			
	References			
	Research Papers			
	Rules and Procedures			
	Schedules			
	Seating Arrangements			
	Self-Assessment Instruments			
	Simulated Experiences			
	Student Contracts			
	Teacher-Made Materials			
	Theme Studies			
	Transcripts			
	Unit Plans			
	Videos			
	Volunteer Experience			
	Work Experience			

From Dorothy M. Campbell et al, How to Develop a Professional Portfolio, 2/e © 2001. Published by Allyn and Bacon, Boston, MA. Copyright © 2001 by Pearson Education. Adapted by permission of the publisher.

Reflection Worksheet

What did I do?

Artifact: _____

What did I learn?

Describe the artifact within its context. _____

_____

Relate the artifact to content or professional standards and learning objectives. _____

_____

_____

How did the artifact impact student learning? _____

_____

_____

What will I do next?

Did the artifact achieve what was intended? _____

_____

Did the artifact meet the learning needs of all my students? _____

_____

What will I change to make the artifact more effective? _____

_____

How will this artifact influence future instruction? _____

_____

Appendix D

Portfolio Design Worksheet

Sketch your page layout inside the box.

Type

Heading font _____   Size _____   Color _____

Subheading font _____   Size _____   Color _____

Text font _____   Size _____   Color _____

Graphics

File type _____   Size _____

Background _____   Color _____

Organizational Elements

Vertical/Horizontal Lines _____   Leading ____   Color _____

Bullets/Numbers _____   Design _____

Other _____

Rubric for Electronic Portfolio Development							
Criteria	**Standard**	**Rating**					**Notes**
		5	**4**	**3**	**2**	**1**	
Selection of Artifacts	All artifacts clearly and directly relate to objectives or standards and document best professional practice						
Reflections	All reflections clearly answer the questions, "What did I do?" "What did I learn?" and "What will I do next?" Reflections relate to objectives or standards						
Structure and navigation	Organization of the portfolio is logical and easy to follow; relationships among portfolio elements are evidenced by workable hyperlinks and navigation elements						
Layout and design	Page layout is logically organized, readable, and follows the principles of good design, including the proper use of color, type size and fonts, contrast, repetition, and proximity; graphics files are the appropriate format and sized to load quickly						
Multimedia	All multimedia, including photos, graphics, video, and audio, are appropriate and are used as artifacts or as enhancements to reflections; multimedia elements do not detract from or interfere with the contents of the portfolio						
Publication	The published portfolio, whether on disk or on the Web, works seamlessly and has no missing graphics, broken hyperlinks, or errors in spelling, punctuation, or grammar						

American Association of School Librarians & Association for Educational Communications and Technology. (1998). *Information Power: Building Partnerships for Learning.* Chicago: American Library Association.

Barrett, H. (1999). *The electronic portfolio development process.* Electronic Portfolios = Multimedia Development + Portfolio Development. [Online]. Available: http://transition.alaska.edu/www/portfolios/EPDevProcess.html 29 April 2003.

Barrett, H. (2000a). Create your own electronic portfolio: Using off-the-shelf software to showcase your own or student work. *Designing and developing standards-based electronic portfolios.* Handout at the meeting of the National Educational Computing Conference, Atlanta, GA.

Barrett, H. (2000b). Electronic portfolio development. *Designing and developing standards-based electronic portfolios.* Handout at the meeting of the National Educational Computing Conference, Atlanta, GA.

Barrett, H. (2000c). *Electronic teaching portfolios: Multimedia skills + portfolio development = powerful professional development.* ERIC ED444 514

Bullock, A. A., & Hawk, P. P. (2001). *Developing a teaching portfolio.* Upper Saddle River, NJ: Merrill Prentice Hall.

Bullough, R., Jr., & Gitlin, A. (1995). *Becoming a student of teaching: Methodologies for exploring self and school context.* New York: Garland.

Burke, K. (1997). *Designing professional portfolios for change.* Pearson, 82.

Campbell, D., Cignetti, P., Melenyzer, B., Nettles, D., & Wyman, R., Jr. (2001). *How to develop a professional portfolio.* Boston: Allyn and Bacon.

Campbell, D., Melenyzer, B., Nettles, D., & Wyman, R., Jr. (2000). *Portfolio and performance assessment in teacher education.* Boston: Allyn and Bacon.

Clandinin, D. J., & Connelly, F. M.(1995). *Teachers' professional knowledge landscapes.* New York: Teachers College.

Clark, D. (2001). *Critical reflection.* [Online]. Available: http://www.nwlink.com/~donclark/hrd/development/reflection.html 5 May 2003.

Clips Ahoy! (2000). *Free clipart island.* [Online]. Available: http://www.clipsahoy.com/ 29 December 2003.

Dice, M. L., & Goldenhersh, B. L. (2002). *How to create a professional electronic portfolio: A guide for the preservice and beginning teacher.* Dubuque, IO: Kendall/Hunt.

Doolittle, P. (1994). *Teacher portfolio assessment.* ERIC ED385608

Educational Multimedia Fair Use Guidelines Development Committee. The Conference on Fair Use. (1996). [On-line]. Available: http://www.utsystem.edu/ogc/intellectualproperty/ccmcguid.htm 5 September 2003.

Grant, C. M. (1996). *Professional development in a technological age: New definitions, old challenges, new resources.* [Online]. Available: http://lsc-net.terc.edu/do.cfm/paper/8089/show/use_set-tech 5 May 2003.

Hill, D. M. (2002). *Electronic portfolios: Teacher candidate development and assessment.* ERIC ED463 261

Kearsley, G. (2003). *Constructivist theory (J. Bruner).* Explorations in Learning & Instruction: The Theory Into Practice Database. [Online]. Available: http://tip.psychology.org/bruner.html 1 September 2003.

Kilbane, C. R., & Milman, N. B. (2003). *The digital teaching portfolio handbook: a how-to guide for educators.* Boston: Allyn and Bacon.

Kimball, M. A. (2003). *The Web portfolio guide: Creating electronic portfolios for the Web.* New York: Longman.

Kolb, D. (2003). *Experience based learning systems, inc.* [Online]. Available: http://www.learningfromexperience.com 1 September 2003

Lamb, A. (2002). *Electronic portfolios: Students, teachers, and life long learners.* [Online]. Available: http://www.eduscapes.com/tap/topic82.htm 29 April 2003.

McKay School of Education. *Electronic portfolios: INTASC standards.* [Online]. Available: http://205.125.10.9/Supporting_files/Standards.htm April 29, 2003.

Miller, D., & Larsen, K. (2003). *Day-by-Day: Professional journaling for library media specialists.* Worthington, OH: Linworth.

Morris, C. (1999). *Timeless typography.* Web Developer's Virtual Library. [Online]. Available: http://www.wdvl.com/Authoring/Design/Pages/typography.html 15 September 2003.

Niederst, J. (2001). *Learning Web design: A beginner's guide to HTML, graphics, and beyond.* Cambridge, MA: O'Reilly.

Public Broadcasting Sysytem. (2003). *Copyright.* TeacherSource. [Online]. Available: http://www.pbs.org/teachersource/copyright/copyright_ed_multi.shtm 5 September 2003.

Schön, D. (1983). *The reflective practitioner: How professionals think in action.* New York: BasicBooks.

Simpson, C. (2001). *Copyright for Schools: A Practical Guide.* Worthington, OH: Linworth.

Stanford University Libraries. (2003). *Copyright & fair use.* [Online]. Available: http://fairuse.stanford.edu/Copyright_and_Fair_Use_Overview/chapter6/index.html 5 September 2003.

Stim, R. (2001). *Getting permission: How to license & clear copyrighted materials online & off.* Berkeley, CA: NOLO.

Tollett, J., Williams, R., & Rohr, D. (2002). *Robin Williams Web design workshop.* Berkeley, CA: Peachpit.

Tyler, R. W. (1949). *Basic principles of curriculum and instruction.* Chicago: University of Chicago.

Vandervelde, J. (2003). *Rubric for electronic teaching portfolio.* A+ Rubric.[Online]. Available: http://www.uni.edu/profdev/rubrics/eportfolio.html 29 April 2003.

Van Wagenen, L., & Hibbard, M. (1998). Building teacher portfolios. *Educational Leadership, 55*(5), 26-29.

Wilcox, B. L., et al. (1997). *Intelligent portfolios for professional development.* ERIC ED 408 250

Williams, R., & Tollett, J. (2000). *The non-designer's Web book.* Berkeley, CA: Peachpit.

Wolf, K. (1996). Developing an effective teaching portfolio. *Educational Leadership, 5* (6), 34-37.
